Section 28

Section 28

A practical guide to the law and its implications

by Madeleine Colvin
with Jane Hawksley

National Council for Civil Liberties

National Council for Civil Liberties
21 Tabard Street
London SE1 4LA

© National Council for Civil Liberties 1989

ISBN 0–946088–32–2

BRITISH LIBRARY CATALOGUING–IN–PUBLICATION DATA

Colvin, Madeleine
    Section 28: a practical guide to the law and
    its implications
    1.Great Britain.   Homosexuality. Policies of
    local authorities.   Law
    I. Title II. National Council for Civil Liberties
    344.105'2536

ISBN 0–946088–32–2

Acknowledgements

The advice and assistance of many people made this book a reality. In particular, thanks to Jan Parker of the Association of London Authorities for her informed and perceptive views of the issues involved and her extensive contribution on local authorities; Caroline Hopper and Steve Wyler at the London Voluntary Service Council for their expertise on the voluntary sector; Dr Gillian Spraggs for her valuable insights into the educational implications of Section 28; Kate Marcus of the Brent Community Law Centre for her advice on legal remedies; Jamie Woolley, solicitor with Sheffield City Council, for permission to draw upon his report; and Terry Munyard for his constructive comments and legal input.

Thanks to Jane Hawksley for her work in editing the manuscript; also to Renée Harris, Nettie Pollard and Camilla Raab for their assistance.

Grateful thanks are also due to the Association of London Authorities for permission to quote its legal Opinions. Finally, we would like to acknowledge the anonymous donation which made the publication of this book possible.

Designed and typeset by Jeff Sanders, ASP Design in ITC Garamond 10 on 11 point Printed by Spider Web

Contents

Introduction

What is Section 28?

Section 28 of the Local Government Act 1988 inserted a new Section 2A into the Local Government Act 1986. You may encounter it under either heading. It states:

(1)   A local authority shall not

   a)   intentionally promote homosexuality or publish material with the intention of promoting homosexuality;

   b)   promote the teaching in any maintained school of the acceptability of homosexuality as a pretended family relationship;

(2)   Nothing in subsection (1) above shall be taken to prohibit the doing of anything for the purpose of treating or preventing the spread of disease.

(3)   In any proceedings in connection with the application of this section a court shall draw such inferences as to the intention of the local authority as may reasonably be drawn from the evidence before it.

The purpose of this book is to examine what this may mean in legal terms, as far as is possible until it has actually been tested in the courts, and later chapters will look closely at the text of these prohibitions and their practical implications. For now, it should be noted that this is the first time this century that a new piece of legislation has been enacted which specifically singles out homosexuality and lesbian and gay lifestyles for disapproval. Opposition to the Section during the time that it was a proposed clause amending the Local Government Act was widespread, not just in Britain but also in the United States and across Europe, and this opposition continues today. Section 28 is widely seen as a major and shameful attack on civil liberties. How did it come about, and what lay behind the Government's decision to adopt this amendment as its own?

History of Section 28

In 1986 the Earl of Halsbury introduced a Private Member's Bill in the House of Lords entitled 'An Act to restrain local authorities from promoting homosexuality'. That Bill applied to local authority activities generally, and to schools in particular, seeking to prevent the 'promotion of homosexuality as an acceptable family relationship'.

Section 28

When it was introduced, the Government Minister responsible, Lord Skelmersdale, took the view that the Bill was unnecessary and open to harmful misinterpretation. Nevertheless, it did pass through the House of Lords and made its way to the House of Commons, adopted by Dame Jill Knight, Conservative MP for Birmingham Edgbaston. It fell because of the announcement of a general election.

Nothing more was heard of the matter until the Local Government Bill was being debated at Committee stage in the House of Commons in December 1987. At this point David Wilshire, one of the Conservative MPs on that Committee, proposed an amendment to the Bill broadly following the Halsbury lines. The amendment was debated on 8 December 1987 in Committee, and this time it was formally adopted by the Government.

The Government maintained that it had taken this U-turn because, it claimed, there was 'growing concern in Parliament and in the country as a whole about the use of ratepayers' money by some local authorities intentionally to promote homosexuality'. However, the 'growing concern in Parliament and in the country as a whole' soon began to look more like the expression of the personal obsessions of a handful of MPs and one or two local authority members, augmented by allegations made in some of the more lurid tabloid newspapers which were subsequently shown to be either complete fabrications or wild distortions.

For example, great and much publicised emphasis was placed on the presence in an Inner London Education Authority teachers' centre (i.e. not a school, but a place to which only teachers had access) of a copy of a children's picture book called *Jenny Lives with Eric and Martin*, which tells the story of an ordinary day in the life of a little girl in Denmark who is being brought up by her gay father Martin and his partner Eric. Illustrated with photographs, it depicts ordinary and mundane family activities like having breakfast and gardening. In one picture the little girl is shown, like countless other children in conventional heterosexual families depicted in countless other children's picture books, as having breakfast in bed in the morning with her father and Eric. This image was seized upon with prurient and salacious outrage by the tabloids, who went on to report, entirely falsely, that the Inner London Education Authority was distributing copies of this book to young children. In fact, the Chief Education Officer of ILEA had ruled that it *not* be made available in school libraries. One copy, of one book, in one teachers' centre, thus entered public mythology as representing a broad educational conspiracy to divert the funds of unwitting ratepayers to the service of some kind of sexual conversion strategy.

MPs made repeated assertions that parents had complained to them of the corruption and indecency to which their children were daily subjected in school, but failed repeatedly to provide any evidence whatsoever to support this. Indeed, Conservative

MP Robin Squires was eventually moved to point out that:

> ... in our discussions on this matter and in our attempts to extract evidence, it appears that most of that evidence arises from one book in one teachers' centre, in one school under one authority. I may be wrong, but I have seen no other evidence. Indeed, as I understand it, that book was kept to help teachers who are occasionally asked to advise pupils who come from homes with gay parents.
> (*Hansard*, House of Commons, 9.3.88, col. 376-7.)

That any government is prepared to support legislation on the basis of evidence which, when examined, turns out to be either non-existent or a complete distortion of the truth, should indeed be a matter of grave concern to all citizens. A number of the allegations about the supposed 'promotion' of homosexuality by Labour-run councils surfaced in the Conservative Party's advertising campaign in the run-up to the 1987 General Election. Large billboards featuring mocked-up books (with significantly red covers) bearing the titles *Young, Gay and Proud* and *Black Lesbian in White America* implied, firstly, that there was something extraordinarily shocking about these books (one a collection of writings by gay teenagers about their lives, the other a collection of academic essays), and secondly that they were somehow part of the alleged 'campaign' to 'sell' homosexuality to impressionable youngsters.

Moreover there seemed to be a remarkable degree of wilful misunderstanding of recent developments in equal opportunity and anti-discrimination policies. Lesbians and gay men are full members of our communities: they pay taxes and rates, and they vote. They are entitled to equal treatment from other people and in the delivery of all public services. Most local authority services, however, are geared to the needs of heterosexual families and are based on the unexamined assumption that the population is uniformly heterosexual. As part of a commitment to their equal opportunity and anti-discrimination policies, some local authorities have set up specialist units: to research where discrimination exists, to offer proposals for policy improvement, to train officers to understand these policies and to encourage lesbian and gay members of the community to make use of services which may never previously have been offered to them, or which they have never before felt able to use.

Positive images policies also came under attack. A positive images policy simply recognises that lesbians and gay men are commonly represented in *distorted* terms (for example, in the lurid manner favoured by some popular newspapers). In a society in which images of homosexual people are almost uniformly negative or wildly inaccurate, a positive images policy takes care to present lesbians and gay men not as in any way superior to heterosexuals, but as people rather than stereotypes. It means, as the Association of London Authorities has put it, encouraging a climate in which lesbians and gay men can be open about themselves, their relationships and their families without fear of attack – in other words, a climate in which everyone can manage their relationships and friendships with integrity, equality and respect.

Government spokespeople in the House of Commons and the House of Lords, however, chose to recast these basically sensible and constructive policies in a manner curiously at odds with their oft-repeated support for equal opportunities. Actually *doing* anything to further equal opportunities and non-discrimination was now, it seemed, to be viewed as the expression of a sinister conspiracy. The Earl of Caithness, leading for the Government in the House of Lords, insisted that:

> What we are seeing in some places is an attempt to sell homosexuality, to ensure that people see it in a favourable light. For this purpose we see all the techniques of modern public relations deployed – entertainments, exhibitions, campaigns, posters. Every local authority service that can possibly be used to put over the message is twisted to serve the same purpose. We see gay library collections, gay consciousness courses for local authority officers and homosexual material produced for children's playgroups [sic]. We have homosexual and lesbian units which comment on every report that is going to the council. Everything then is done to glamorise homosexuality to make all aspects of homosexuality seem attractive. It is this hard sell of homosexuality that is so worrying... I therefore argue that the core of the mischief that we are concerned with is something very akin to a public relations campaign... I therefore think that it is correct to use the vocabulary of the advertising trade to describe it.

There is an extraordinary mental jump here, since no one would imagine for a moment that local authority support of, say, a Greek or German cultural festival, or of posters condemning discrimination against Greeks or Germans, was in fact a promotional campaign designed to persuade people to rush to take out Greek or German citizenship.

Eventually it turned out that it was not so much a series of activities (whether real or imagined), but of imputed *intentions,* which the Government sought to ban. Months into the debate the Earl of Caithness in fact said: 'Some local authorities have been concerned to ensure that the services provided by the councils serve the needs of homosexuals as much as the needs of the community [sic]. There can be no objection to such an aim'. But the arguments for Section 28 were all based on the unsubstantiated assertion that behind such concern lay the suspect intention of 'some local authorities' to mount a promotional campaign to 'sell' homosexuality. The extreme danger of this is that almost any activity in support of equal opportunities, or to 'ensure that the services provided by the councils serve the needs of homosexuals as much as the needs of the community', can, it seems, be cited as evidence of this supposed intention.

Why have we produced this book?

Section 28 is an extraordinarily badly-drafted piece of legislation, and some have argued that it is unlikely ever to be used to any effect because of its narrow scope and the difficulties of its interpretation. But it is also a very dangerous piece of legislation, because as long as these difficulties of interpretation remain, there is the very real likelihood that, *without cases ever coming to court*, Section 28 will be both misunderstood and misinterpreted, and used to justify acts and decisions which result in censorship and discrimination.

Since the Section came into force on 24 May 1988, there have been several examples of this.

- In May 1988, East Sussex County Council banned the distribution of a National Youth Bureau directory in its schools on the grounds that it infringed Section 28. The directory, containing over a hundred projects or organisations offering voluntary work opportunities for young people, listed a gay and lesbian organisation which sought volunteers over the age of 14 'with a positive attitude to their sexuality'.

- On 23 September 1988, a production of *Trapped in Time*, due to be performed by the Avon Touring Theatre Company in a secondary school, was cancelled by the school's head teacher. The play, which examines the way different people have been represented in history, is intended as a serious educational piece of theatre challenging young people to think about issues of racism, sexism and sexuality. It includes a short scene called 'Queen Victoria's Coming Out', in which one of the characters tells his friends that he is gay. In banning the play, the head teacher expressed concern that he might be in breach of Section 28 if he allowed the performance to go ahead.

- Student unions have also been subject to restrictions, allegedly under Section 28. In January 1988 the Director of the City of Leeds College of Music banned the students' Gay and Lesbian Society from meeting on college premises. In Scotland, the Deputy Director of Education at Strathclyde wrote to all Colleges of Further Education in April

1988 stating that grants to student associations would be withheld unless they agreed to cease all lesbian and gay related activities. In August 1988 Essex County Council issued a directive to all principals of Further Education Colleges instructing them not to allow lesbian or gay groups to meet in colleges or in any other council-owned building.

There are forceful legal arguments for saying that none of these banned activities in fact actually contravenes Section 28.

The purpose of this book is to provide information and guidance so that similar decisions are not made in legal error and so that they can be challenged when they are. In particular, it seeks to assist local authorities in maintaining equal opportunity policies and practices which include lesbians and gay men; to provide assurance to professionals – such as teachers and youth workers – that they may continue to deal with issues to do with homosexuality in a constructive, informed and balanced way; to help voluntary organisations working against all forms of discrimination to negotiate with local authorities over matters affected by Section 28, and to give individuals and organisations the knowledge with which they might challenge inaccurate interpretations of the new law.

This book can be read straight through, but we also realise that many readers will be busy professionals who may want to turn directly to the chapters which have a bearing on their own work. For this reason we have repeated some core principles in each chapter. We recommend, however, that *everyone* reads Chapter One, Legal Overview, and Chapter Five, Legal Challenges, along with their specialist chapter.

Following the legal and practical advice given in this book cannot be a *guarantee* against a legal challenge. It does, however, provide a sound legal framework within which local authorities can continue with or initiate good practice, and which will help them to avoid being panicked into inappropriate and destructive decisions.

It is important to remember that Section 28 has been implicated in recent and increasingly virulent eruptions of anti-gay and anti-lesbian feeling and action, much of it promoted by parts of the media. Section 28 itself has been quite mistakenly seen as actually legalising discrimination against lesbians and gay men. Its mere existence has raised considerable concern about standards of tolerance in a civilised society. Some of these issues are discussed more fully in the conclusion to this book. It is to be hoped that the debate about Section 28 will serve to widen the discussion and deepen the level of understanding about how discrimination operates. This book is intended to play a part in that debate.

Chapter One
Legal overview

What kind of law is Section 28?

Section 28 creates a **civil** law as opposed to a **criminal** law. It regulates what a local authority may not do, but does not mean that a local authority (or anyone else) is subject to punishment by the criminal courts. The two main sources of law in Britain are:

(1) **Acts of Parliament**

(2) Decisions made by judges in court cases, which then create precedents for later cases. This is called **judge-made law, case law,** or **common law**.

Section 28 began as an amendment tabled by David Wilshire MP to insert a new clause into the Government's Local Government Bill. Most Acts of Parliament start as Bills introduced by the government of the day. As a Bill goes through the several parliamentary stages it may be subject to amendment. The success of such amendments largely depends on whether the government gives support, as it did with Section 28.

It is the **courts** which decide, in practice, how Acts of Parliament should be interpreted. If a person, or government department, claims that an Act means one thing and someone else maintains that it means another, it is for the court to decide what it means. This is the process of arriving at a clear meaning of the law.

In order to do this the wording of the law is looked at very carefully. The words in the law must be given their *ordinary* and *natural* meaning, but this is sometimes difficult to do, and we shall see later on how this difficulty affects Section 28. Once the courts have interpreted a law, however, this interpretation is binding on all subsequent cases where the new law applies.

To whom does it apply?

Section 28 can only be invoked against a **local authority**. It cannot be used against individuals or companies or even against other publicly funded bodies like the Arts Council, the British Film Institute, the BBC or the Health Education Authority. Nothing that these bodies do is made illegal by the Section. Despite widespread and sloppy reporting that it is now illegal for a publishing company to publish gay books or for a theatre to put on gay plays, this is categorically *not true*. Problems with Section 28 could only arise if the publisher or theatre were *funded* by a local authority – and even then the matter is not at all straightforward, as we shall see.

Section 28

How would it be invoked?

Someone would have to bring a case against a local authority alleging that it had done something in breach of Section 28 of the Local Government Act 1988. Any ratepayer can, in theory, take their local authority to the High Court by applying for a **Judicial Review** of the action or decision they think might be in breach of the Section. The High Court's function here is to make a decision about whether the local authority has or has not acted illegally in the matter under question. The High Court cannot punish the local authority (for example, by fining it) if it is found to have acted illegally, but it can make an **injunction** restraining the local authority from carrying on with its action.

There is another situation in which Section 28 might be invoked. The **District Auditor**, who is the official appointed to oversee local authority finances, could take the view that local councillors have exceeded their legal powers in, for example, giving a grant to a gay theatre company. The District Auditor would then instruct councillors to cease the expenditure. If they were to refuse, the councillors could be surcharged. If this were to happen the councillors would be disbarred from holding public office for a certain period.

Difficulties of interpretation

As we have seen, it is the courts which decide how the law should be interpreted. At the time of publication no case has been brought under Section 28 and therefore no court has made a judgment about how the Section should apply. In addition, it is generally recognised that Section 28 is an obscure and badly-drafted piece of legislation, containing words which are ambiguous and uncertain in their meaning. For example, what is meant by the phrase **'a pretended family relationship'**? How do we arrive at a definition of **'promote'**, a key word in the Section but one which has no single and unambiguous meaning in general use? In cases where the meaning of words in a piece of legislation is as unclear as this, the courts usually resort to defining the 'mischief' which is intended to be affected by the new law. But in the case of Section 28 this is likely to be as difficult as interpreting the actual words, as we shall see.

Written legal Opinions

Until the Section has been tested in the courts, we must rely upon the opinions of senior and experienced lawyers as to what it means, what is permissible under the law and what is now illegal. It is for this reason that comprehensive legal 'Opinions' have been sought: the Association of London Authorities (ALA) commissioned an Opinion from Michael Barnes QC on the general legal effect of Section 28; and in

June 1988 the ALA and National Council for Civil Liberties jointly commissioned an Opinion from Lord Gifford QC on the particular implications of the Section for education. (Lord Gifford's Opinion was produced jointly with his junior Terry Munyard.) These two legal Opinions provide the basis for what follows in this book. Written legal Opinions have no official status and are not documents which are used in court. They contain the informed opinion of experienced senior lawyers on the *likely interpretation* that the courts will place on the law. In the absence of a court decision as to interpretation, a legal Opinion is the next best form of guidance on how the law should be viewed.

Provisions of Section 28

Let us now look more closely at what Section 28 says:

Local Government Act 1988

28 – (1) The following section shall be inserted after section 2 of the Local Government Act 1986 (prohibition of political publicity) –

2A – (1) A local authority shall not:

   (a) intentionally promote homosexuality or publish material with the intention of promoting homosexuality;

   (b) promote the teaching in any maintained school of the acceptability of homosexuality as a pretended family relationship.

(2) Nothing in subsection (1) above shall be taken to prohibit the doing of anything for the purpose of treating or preventing the spread of disease.

(3) In any proceedings in connection with the application of this section a court shall draw such inferences as to the intention of the local authority as may reasonably be drawn from the evidence before it.

(4) In subsection (1) (b) above "maintained school" means, –

   (a) in England and Wales, a county school, voluntary school, nursery school or special school, within the meaning of the Education Act 1944; and

   (b) in Scotland, a public school, nursery school or special school, within the meaning of the Education (Scotland) Act 1980.

(2) This section shall come into force at the end of the period of two months beginning with the day on which this Act is passed.

The Section therefore introduces three prohibitions on local authorities:

1. **That a local authority shall not intentionally promote homosexuality.**

2. **That a local authority shall not publish material with the intention of promoting homosexuality; and**

3. **That a local authority shall not promote the teaching in any maintained school of the acceptability of homosexuality as a pretended family relationship.**

Remember that Section 28 is only about what a *local authority* can and cannot do. Although other organisations and individuals may be indirectly affected by the prohibitions – for example, by having local authority grant-aid rescinded on the grounds of Section 28 – they are not bound in law to abide by them.

But even in the case of local authorities, the situation is not clear cut. For example, how do these prohibitions fit in with the *other* legal obligations of local authorities?

There is already a problem here, because there is a basic legal principle of **'equal treatment'** which governs local authorities in the way they carry out all their activities. Section 28 cannot operate to prejudice this overall principle, which means that Section 28 cannot operate to 'override' or 'cancel' or even 'weaken' the principle of equal treatment.

The duty of equal treatment

In general terms, a local authority has a duty to carry out its duties and provide services without **discriminating between individuals or groups of individuals.**

This general principle is based on the wording of the various statutes from which local authorities derive their powers. For example, in the case of public libraries, **Section 7** of the **Public Libraries and Museums Act 1964** provides that:

> it shall be the duty of every library authority to provide a comprehensive
> and efficient library service for all persons desiring to make use thereof.

The statutes governing local authorities' powers and duties in the fields of social services, housing, the making of grants and so on all contain words which require local authorities to have regard to the needs of the inhabitants of their area.

Section 28 has not altered or amended this basic duty of local authorities. It therefore follows that the Section cannot *require* local authorities to exercise any of their functions in a way which is detrimental to or which discriminates against a particular group of people – for example, people who identify themselves or who are identified by others as lesbians and gay men; nor can it *justify* the exercising of their functions in a detrimental or discriminatory manner. You should note that this point has been emphasised in the government circular which relates to Section 28, **Circular 12/88**.

(For the legal significance of government circulars, see p. 15; for the text of this circular, see Appendix Three, p. 73.)

The principle of equal treatment in the European Convention on Human Rights

The concept of 'equal treatment' is also contained in the European Convention on Human Rights. This Convention is an international treaty ratified by a number of states including the United Kingdom, setting out the fundamental civil and political rights of individuals which must be safeguarded by those states who are its signatories. **Article 14** provides that the enjoyments, rights and freedoms set out in the Convention shall be secured 'without discrimination on any ground such as sex, race, colour ... or other status'.

These words are wide enough to prevent discrimination against people on the ground of their sexual orientation. Although the Convention is not part of domestic law and cannot itself be enforced through the British courts, our courts can properly assume that **Parliament did not intend a statute to be construed in a way which would violate the obligations of the United Kingdom under the Convention.** (For more discussion of the European Convention, see p. 60).

Having made this general point, it is important to examine the interpretation of key words and phrases in the text of Section 28.

Interpretation of key words

Several key words are integral to the three prohibitions contained in Section 28. What meaning is likely to be given them by the courts? This is an important question, because however difficult fixing their meaning might prove to be, the courts will be reluctant to reach the conclusion that words or phrases are either legally meaningless or without any effect at all. It must therefore be expected that the courts will attempt to construe some meaning from the context in which the words appear. It is with this in mind that the legal Opinions have offered the following interpretations as being most likely.

Section 28

a) 'Promote homosexuality'

In its ordinary meaning *homosexuality* connotes an abstract *concept* of sexual attraction between people of the same sex. Therefore in a strict sense it does not include sexual acts between persons of the same gender. However it is apparent that 'homosexuality' is *not* used exclusively in its ordinary sense in Section 28. For example, the Section implies that 'homosexuality' might be represented as a '...family relationship'. The courts are therefore likely to construe it as having a wider meaning which includes sexual acts and relationships.

The word *promote* underpins Section 28. It was, therefore, the focus of much debate, both in Parliament and outside. In the absence of any definition in the Act itself, the courts are likely to seek assistance from:

- the dictionary definition of the word
- other legislation in which it is used.

For example, it is important that the word 'promote' occurs also in Section 27 of the **Local Government Act 1988**, which deals with local authority publicity. Section 27 says that in determining whether material published by local authorities falls within the prohibition against political publicity regard shall be had, among other things, to whether the material

> promotes or opposes a point of view on a question of political controversy which is identifiable as the view of one political party and not of another.

In that section the word 'promote' clearly means pushing a point of view with the intention of persuading people to adopt it.

The concept of 'promotion' is also familiar in the field of company law, where it is used to describe the putting out of a company prospectus in order to persuade the public to purchase shares. Taking these factors into account, Lord Gifford concluded in his written Opinion that:

> 'promote homosexuality' involves active advocacy directed by local authorities towards individuals in order to persuade them to become homosexual, or to experiment with homosexual relationships.

The advocacy may be direct or indirect: it could take the form of direct exhortation; or indirect presentation of homosexuality aimed at inducing people to try it who otherwise would not. But whether direct or indirect, there must be *active persuasion* by the local authority before Section 28 is breached.

This is in line with the way the Government has used the word 'promote' in a variety of statements about Section 28, where it has been maintained that the intention of the Section is to prevent the 'hard sell' of homosexuality.

b) 'Intentionally'

This is another key word. The Government amended the original draft of Section 28 to include the word 'intentionally' in order to put beyond doubt that **it is the local authority's intention which is crucial in deciding whether it has acted unlawfully. Only if a local authority *intended* to 'promote homosexuality' will it fall foul of the law.**

Intention, of course, is a state of mind. If action is taken with the *motive* or *desire* of bringing about a particular result, that result is intended. Even in the absence of an explicit motive, a result may still be intended if the action is taken knowing that it is *highly likely* that such a result will happen. On the other hand, if there is only a *slight risk* that the result will happen and there is no *wish* that it should do so, then the result cannot be said to be intended.

Section 28 means that local authorities are now bound to consider whether or not their decisions or actions intentionally 'promote homosexuality' in the sense as defined above. In doing so, they must look fully at the *likely implications* of any decision or action. *Not wishing* to promote homosexuality does not necessarily fulfil their obligations. In Chapter Two, p. 24, there is an outline of a step-by-step approach that should be taken by local authorities in reaching decisions which may be affected by Section 28.

How will a local authority's 'intention' be determined? A conclusion about the authority's intention will be drawn from the decisions of its committees, the reports submitted to those committees and from any material actually published by the authority. We will examine this in detail in Chapter Two, pp. 23-29, where we will discuss the role of local authority officers' reports and council resolutions.

In determining the intention of a corporate body (i.e. a council committee) the courts will not try to probe the minds of individual councillors or examine individual contributions to debates. However, the *public statement*s of council leaders or committee chairs *could* be put before the court as evidence of the intention of the local authority.

c) 'Pretended family relationship'

The phrase 'pretended family relationship' creates obvious linguistic difficulties, since 'homosexuality' is a form of sexuality and not a 'family relationship'. The word 'pretended' adds little to the sense, except to emphasise Parliament's view that a homosexual family relationship is not a real family relationship.

Section 28

The subsection appears to prohibit local authorities from advocating, either directly or indirectly, that pupils should be taught, at least as part of their curriculum, that a homosexual family relationship is acceptable as being on a par with a heterosexual family relationship. (For further discussion of this, see Chapter Four.)

So how does this affect existing activities?

It is probably true to say that local authorities have never actually had the power to 'promote homosexuality' in the sense defined above – let alone have ever done so. Their decisions and activities in, for example, supporting lesbian and gay advice agencies, have been undertaken under one or more of the legal powers to fund voluntary organisations as part of their general duties (see Chapter Two). Local authorities will continue to be able to use these statutory powers so long as the outcome is not to 'promote homosexuality' in the sense defined above. It is therefore not surprising that Michael Barnes in his legal Opinion formed the view that **'it is open to serious doubt whether [Section 28] will render unlawful many decisions or actions [of local authorities] presently lawful.'** Taking account of the legal interpretation of key words and phrases in Section 28, it is likely that the courts would take the view that the Section prohibits local authorities from doing the things listed below.

Prohibitions

Local authorities must not:

- Make a decision or take an action directed towards individuals which is intended to persuade them to become homosexual, or to experiment with homosexual relationships, or which is highly likely to do so.

- Publish material directed towards individuals which is intended to persuade them to become homosexual, or to experiment with homosexual relationships, or which is highly likely to do so.

- Directly or indirectly advocate that pupils should be taught, at least as a regular part of their curriculum, that a homosexual family relationship is acceptable as being on a par with a heterosexual family relationship.

Not prohibited

As long as a local authority does not intend to 'promote homosexuality', it will continue to be lawful to undertake, for example, the following functions:

- To discourage discrimination against lesbians and gay men on the ground of their sexuality.

- To give assistance and support to agencies which give information, advice and assistance to, or concerning, lesbians and gay men.

- To give support and provide facilities for the arts generally, including those involving homosexual themes.

- To provide policy and guidance to schools on the school curriculum, including sex education which advocates a balanced and objective discussion of homosexuality.

For more discussion of the implications of Section 28 for equal opportunity policies and specific local authority services, see Chapter Two.

Apart from considering the actual words and phrases used in the Section, there is another way that local authorities can reasonably proceed when trying to judge which actions and decisions are made unlawful by the new law and which are not. This is by looking at the government circulars and statements which refer to Section 28.

Government circulars and statements

When the courts are asked to interpret new legislation they primarily consider the actual wording of the statute itself. By tradition, they are normally restricted from using, for example, government circulars and parliamentary debates as aids to interpretation. This rule is based on the notion of the separation of powers between legislators and the judiciary. However, it is the view of the author of the leading work on statutory interpretation that 'Despite (this) exclusionary rule, the court retains overall control of its procedure, and if it thinks fit will disregard the rule' (see *Statutory Interpretation* p. 533, by Francis Bennion, 1984). He points out that the parliamentary history of a Bill has been cited in at least 16 recorded cases.

In any event, until there is an interpretation laid down by the court, it would be reasonable for local authorities to consider statements in *Hansard* and government circulars for the following reasons:

Section 28

a) As mentioned earlier, the District Auditor can enquire into the lawfulness of items of expenditure. In theory, this means that councillors could be surcharged and subsequently disbarred from office. But the law specifically states that no surcharging of councillors is to take place if 'the person responsible for any such expenditure acted reasonably or in the belief that the expenditure was authorised by law' (**Section 90 (3), Local Government Finance Act 1982**). It is therefore important that councillors and officers equip themselves with the best possible understanding of what Section 28 was intended by its legislators to deal with and what the words in it were intended to mean. One of the best ways they have of understanding this is through government statements and circulars.

b) The signed minutes of the authority are admissible evidence in court, and if a report from officers is attached which refers to *Hansard* or relevant circulars, it will demonstrate 'good faith' on the part of the council in how it arrived at its decision. It is also a convenient way of ensuring that these matters are brought to the court's attention, and puts in the minds of the judiciary the Government's views on how the Section should be interpreted.

Government circulars

Government circulars are issued by the relevant government department in order to give guidance on policy and practice in relation to a piece of legislation. The circulars do not have the force of law that a statute does; they are not binding. This means that the advice or guidance given in them does not necessarily have to be followed. However, it is undoubtedly important for local authorities to take account of them in determining what they may legitimately do.

Government statements

Statements made by government ministers during the course of a bill's passage through parliament are an important guide to the way that the Government considers that the law should be interpreted. In addition, there have been several letters written by ministers clarifying the Government's view of Section 28. Some of these letters are reproduced in Appendix Four.

Chapter Two
Implications for local authorities

Section 28 is directed at local authorities. This chapter examines the likely implications of the Section on the exercise by local authorities of their functions of

- service provision
- grant-aiding and
- as employers.

As pointed out in Chapter One, uncertainty as to the legal meaning of Section 28 has led to serious misunderstanding about what local authorities can and can't do under the new law. Local authorities have a wide range of duties and legal obligations to fulfil towards their ratepayers and local population – for example, in the fields of education, social services, housing and recreation – and it is important that local authority officers and councillors be accurately informed so that neither misinterpretation nor straightforward prejudice be allowed to create a kind of 'sexual apartheid' which would operate against the fulfilment of these obligations.

Does Section 28 alter the duty of local authorities to provide equal treatment?

No. As was discussed on p. 10, this basic but important principle, that local authorities are statutorily bound *not* to discriminate in the provision of services between individuals or groups in the community, is not altered by Section 28. As the Local Government Minister, Michael Howard MP, assured Parliament:

> As it stands Clause 27 [Section 28] will not provide any justification for a local authority discriminating against homosexuals.
> (*Hansard*, 15.12.87, col. 1020.)

This has been reinforced by **Circular 12/88**, issued by the Department of Environment on 20 May 1988 to provide general guidance on the provisions of the Local Government Act 1988. In relation to Section 28 the Circular says:

> Local authorities will not be prevented by this section from offering the full range of services to homosexuals on the same basis as to all their inhabitants. So long as they are not setting out to promote homosexuality they may, for example, include in their public libraries books and periodicals about homosexuality or written by homosexuals, and fund theatre and other arts events which may include homosexual themes.
> (For the full text of this Circular see Appendix Three, p. 73.)

Section 28

Will Section 28 affect equal opportunity policies?

No. Many local authorities have adopted equal opportunity policies and practices both as employers and in the services they provide to the public. In order to implement these policies effectively, some local authorities have begun to investigate the situation of various targeted groups in their communities recognised as having been excluded from previous decision making and policy planning, to see whether these sections of the public have needs which have been wrongly ignored in the provision of public services to date.

To this end local authorities have set up specialist posts and structures such as committees, working parties or officers with special responsibilities for these groups. The aim is to correct a previously existing imbalance and to ensure that all citizens henceforth have equal access to the facilities and services to which they are entitled.

This course of action is consistent with the duty of equal treatment, and remains lawful despite Section 28. It is, however, a course of action which has been sensationally misinterpreted by the media when it has included attempts to investigate and correct the exclusion of people who are not heterosexual from services which the local authority is statutorily obliged to make available to all. Note that in the House of Lords, the Earl of Caithness said:

> The Clause is not about stopping local authorities providing services to homosexuals. Some local authorities have tried to ensure that the services provided ... serve the needs of homosexuals as much as the need of the community. There can be no objection to such an aim.
> (*Hansard*, House of Lords, 2.2.88, col. 1017.)

Local authorities have also adopted conscious equal opportunities policies in their role as employers, in order to eliminate discrimination against job applicants or existing employees because of their sex, race, sexual preference or disability. If such a policy forbids discrimination on grounds of sexual preference, is it prohibited by Section 28?

The legal Opinion of Michael Barnes QC is that it is not prohibited: 'we do not consider that discouraging forms of discrimination against homosexuals on the ground of their homosexuality is to be equated with the promotion of homosexuality.'

This view is not only confirmed in ministerial statements (see p. 67) but also by Government action. It is perhaps ironic that at the same time as Section 28 was being enacted, it was reported that the Department of the Environment is one of seven ministries leading an 'equality of opportunity' initiative to end staff discrimination against, and harassment of, gay and lesbian civil servants.

The Cabinet Office warning to staff is that:

> Discrimination on the grounds of sexual orientation is not tolerated and any harassment from such a cause will be considered an offence under the disciplinary rules.

The Cabinet Office also made a point of praising the Department of Education for running two staff seminars on equality of opportunity for homosexuals (*Guardian*, 27 April 1988).

Summary

Section 28 does not prevent local authorities from:

- Having equal opportunity policies which forbid discrimination against lesbians and gay men.

- Implementing such policies in all areas, including personnel, service delivery and grant-aid.

- Opposing discrimination against lesbians and gay men in all areas.

- Taking steps to ensure that all council departments are as responsive to the needs of lesbians and gay men as they are to the rest of the public.

Such decisions and actions are consistent with the local authority serving *all* its inhabitants.

Section 28

Implications for specific services

On page 15 we looked at what local authorities will be entitled to continue to do in general terms. The following section reviews the position with regard to the following specific services:

- Personnel
- Arts and Theatres
- Libraries
- Housing
- Social Services
- Licensing and Premises

The grant-aiding of voluntary organisations and issues to do with education are dealt with in Chapters Three and Four.

Personnel

Equal opportunity policies forbidding discrimination against people who identify themselves, or who are identified by others, as gay or lesbian will continue to be lawful and desirable. For example, disciplinary and grievance procedures which seek to protect people from harassment because of their sexuality are not affected by Section 28.

The recruitment of gay and lesbian workers on the basis of their own understanding of other gays and lesbians is lawful where it improves any service catering specifically for gays and lesbians.

The criteria on which people are employed to work with children or young people should remain the same whether those people are heterosexual or gay. The only relevant criteria are those which establish objectively that the particular worker concerned is likely to harm the interests of the young person, and those criteria should be *identical* regardless of whether the worker is heterosexual or gay.

Arts and Theatres

The **DoE Circular 12/88** states that:

> So long as [authorities] are not setting out to promote homosexuality, they may ... fund theatre and other arts events which may include homosexual themes.

Local authorities may continue to give access to council venues or council-funded venues for such events and provide resources to writers, artists or performers of material which deals sympathetically with lesbian and gay themes. However, a local authority which backed a series of plays with lesbian and gay themes and did not also back similar kinds of series concerning other social groups, might expect to be the focus of enquiries as to its intentions.

Following representations made to him as a consequence of anxiety in the arts world as to the implications of Section 28 the Minister for the Arts, Richard Luce, stated in a letter to the Association of Metropolitan Authorities:

> If, for example, an authority clearly had a policy of seeking to bring the work of all sorts of artists and playwrights before the public and from time to time put on exhibitions or plays for this purpose, the fact that the artists concerned include some who were homosexual would not put the local authority at risk under the Section. The local authority's intention would clearly be the promotion of art rather than the promotion of homosexuality.

(See also theatre groups in schools, p. 53. For the legal status of government statements and circulars, see pp. 15-16.)

Gay Pride Weeks were the focus of particular attention during the parliamentary debates on Section 28 and local authority involvement in such events is likely to be subjected to close scrutiny. Here, once more, it is the purpose and intention behind the local authority's decision which is crucial. When reviewing a grant application for a Gay Pride Week, the local authority will need to satisfy itself that the aim of the event is not to persuade people to become homosexual, or that it is not a highly likely consequence of the event that people will be persuaded to become homosexual.

At the time of the North London 'Lesbian Strength and Gay Pride' Week in June 1988, the four Leaders of the London boroughs which assisted with funding made it clear that support was being given as part of their equal opportunities policies 'to assist and support communities in the planning and organising of cultural events and festivals'. It is worth remembering in this context that, for example, support for a Chilean or Greek festival celebrating Chilean or Greek culture is unlikely to be interpreted as persuasion to become Chilean or Greek, and it would be advisable for local authorities to detail assistance given to other groups for similar events.

Libraries

Local authorities have a duty to provide a comprehensive library service (see p. 10). As regards Section 28, the **DoE Circular 12/88** states:

> So long as [authorities] are not setting out to promote homosexuality, they may, for example, include in their public libraries books and periodicals about homosexuality or written by homosexuals ...

It would appear from legal Opinions obtained that a library is entitled to catalogue and display such books and materials under a gay/lesbian heading, if it so wishes. Local authorities may also encourage libraries to make their community facilities available to all sections of the community whatever their sexual preference.

Housing

Section 28 does not prohibit a local authority adopting policies which ensure that lesbians and gay men are not discriminated against in the provision of public housing. An equal treatment policy which includes the principle that joint tenants of the same sex are to be treated in the same way as joint tenants of the opposite sex is not unlawful; neither is a policy which holds that lesbian and gay partners may succeed to tenancies in the same way as heterosexual couples. A housing policy which recognises that harassment of lesbians and gay men on the grounds of their sexuality takes place, and that as a consequence they may need re-housing, is also not unlawful.

Social Services

Counselling: The Government has repeatedly confirmed that Section 28 is not intended to limit the personal support and counselling services which a local authority may provide or fund (see, for example, several ministerial statements under the heading 'Voluntary Organisations' in Appendix Three).

Social workers may continue to offer counselling to all, regardless of their sexuality, and to refer people who identify as lesbian or gay to specialist counselling services if these services are required.

Child custody, fostering and adoption: It is clear from DSS guidance in relation to other child-related legislation (for example, see *Guide for Guardians Ad Litem in the Juvenile Court,* DHSS, 1984) that the sexual orientation of a parent(s) will never be a proper basis for automatically rejecting that parent(s) as having custody of a child. Section 28 does not affect the position that such cases must be considered on their individual merits and prejudice should not be allowed to stand in the way of a proper professional judgment. The same is true for cases of fostering and adoption.

Local authorities may continue to adopt a policy that there should be no general rule discriminating against applicants on the grounds of their declared or known sexual orientation.

Social workers who are called upon to advise courts on child custody cases should continue to advise *solely* on the basis of what is considered to be in the best interests of the child.

Licensing and Premises

The carrying out of licensing functions by local authorities is unlikely to be affected by Section 28 (see also ministerial statements on p. 69).

The provision of either:
- short-term meeting or performance space or
- longer-term premises

by local authorities to individuals or groups of people identified as lesbians or gay men continues to be lawful in accordance with the authority's duty of equal treatment and any specific equal opportunities policy (see also p. 28 on the question of 'intention' to promote homosexuality and the granting of meeting facilities).

How should a local authority proceed with its decisions and actions?

Despite the best opinions that can be given as to the legality of all the above decisions and actions, it is important to stress here once more that until Section 28 has been tested formally in the courts, there can be no *guarantee* against a legal challenge. A local authority, acting in good faith that it is proceeding lawfully, should at the present time nonetheless take steps to ensure that it is as little open to challenge as it can be and that, if a challenge is brought, the court will have in front of it a record of the clear intentions of the local authority and of the steps that were taken to ensure that, as far as possible, it made its decisions and took actions in line with what it had an obligation to do and was empowered to do.

Officers' reports

Experience of legal challenges on other issues has shown that officers' reports play a major role in assessing whether a local authority has acted lawfully. How decisions are justified and presented in reports is vital.

Both officers in their reports and councillors in their deliberations should therefore follow three steps when taking any decisions or actions which may be affected by Section 28.

The local authority should:

Step 1:

- Satisfy itself that there are **relevant powers** authorising what is proposed. For example, grant-aid may be authorised under section 137 of the Local Government Act 1972.

Step 2:

- Satisfy itself that there are **relevant facts** which make it reasonable and desirable to exercise those powers – for example, that the proposed action is in line with the authority's equal opportunities policy.

Step 3:

- Consider **whether what is proposed contravenes any of the three prohibitions** set out in Section 28 – for example, by discussing whether it is highly likely that homosexuality will be promoted as a result of supporting the proposal. If it is decided that it is not highly likely, the local authority should make it clear that it has considered the matter to its own satisfaction and that it is not its intention to promote homosexuality.

Let us examine these steps in more detail:

Step 1: Are there existing statutory powers authorising this act or decision?

A first and necessary step in considering any decision or action is for an authority to satisfy itself that there are statutory powers authorising what is proposed. There are both *general* and *specific* powers and duties which can authorise and justify policies and actions which address lesbian and gay equality.

General powers include the powers to provide information, conduct research, buy and sell land and so on. Most of these are to be found in the Local Government Act 1972.

Specific powers are to do with particular services: for example, they are the powers and duties of authorities in housing, education or social services. There are many

Acts of Parliament from which authorities derive their powers and functions, and they vary depending on the type of authority – for example, whether it is a London borough, district or county council and whether it is in England, Wales or Scotland (see *Opening the Town Hall Door: an introduction to local government* by Jane Hutt, NCVO 1988). It is beyond the scope of this book to cite a power for every situation, so the following list draws attention only to the most relevant.

The Local Government Act 1972

Section 111:

This gives local authorities power to do anything:

> calculated to facilitate, or which is conducive or incidental to, the discharge of any of their functions.

It is not an independent power and must be used in conjunction with others – for example, Section 137 of the same Act in relation to grant-aiding a voluntary organisation.

Section 111 can also be used to cover part of the expenditure on special units, such as a lesbian and gay unit, or on specialist staff, to the extent that they are incidental to other functions – for example, helping other departments of the authority to carry out their functions in personnel, housing, etc. Powers to co-opt community representatives to lesbian and gay committees, sub-committees, or working parties are also contained in the Act.

Sections 142 (1) and 142 (2) (a) and (b)

These contain powers regarding access to information and the publication of information, and the arrangement of lectures, discussions and exhibitions on local government matters.

Section 145

This contains a general power for the provision of entertainments, including spending on concerts, dances, music festivals, operatic or dramatic societies, bonfires and so on.

The Local Government (Miscellaneous Provisions) Act 1976

Section 19

This contains powers to provide recreational facilities, premises and staff and the power to fund sporting events.

The Public Libraries and Museums Act 1964

Section 4

This contains a general duty to provide a comprehensive library service adequate to meet both general and specialist requirements of all persons.

Section 9

This contains a power to contribute to the provision of library facilities to the public by another library authority or by any other person. This can be used to fund the establishment of specialist library facilities.

Public Health (Control of Diseases) Act 1984

Section 54

This contains a power to arrange the publication of information about health and disease. This information can include pictures or films. It is worth noting that the DoE Government Circular 12/88 states in relation to subsection 2A(2) of Section 28 that

> activities in the counselling, health care and health education fields undertaken for the purpose of treating or preventing the spread of disease, including AIDS, will not be prohibited. This includes activities concerned exclusively with the needs of homosexuals.

Powers relevant to grant-aid

There are many statutory powers under which local authorities may provide grant-aid to voluntary organisations, including lesbian and gay projects. There are specific Acts relating to particular services – for example, a hostel for people made homeless as a result of harassment because of their sexual orientation could be funded under **Section 58** of the **Housing Act 1985.**

Projects concerned more generally with the collection and dissemination of information about the needs of lesbians and gay men come under the classification 'research', and may be funded under **Section 141** of the **Local Government Act** (see above) or **Section 88** of the **Local Government Act 1985. Section 142** of the **1972 Act** (see above) may also be relevant.

Projects which are not concerned with either service provision, information or research may be funded under **Section 137** of the **Local Government Act 1972** which allows local authorities to spend on schemes of general benefit to the area. (However, amendments contained in the Government's Local Government and Housing Bill 1989 will severely restrict this power and are likely to result in a serious reduction of local authority funding for voluntary organisations.) A voluntary organisation may be funded to provide information on, for example, homosexuals and AIDS under the **Public Health (Control of Disease) Act 1984**. For lesbian and gay youth projects, social services and educational powers of the local authority are likely to be relevant.

Step 2: Is it reasonable and appropriate to exercise the powers?

Once a statutory power has been identified for what is proposed, consideration should be given as to whether there are *relevant factors* which make it both reasonable and appropriate that the authority exercise that power – for example, that there is a need to be met and the proposal falls within the local authority's equal opportunity policy.

In this respect, it will generally be advisable for officers' reports to set out:

- what *general* provision there is in the area under consideration which includes provision for lesbians and gay men.

- what *special* provision there is in the area under consideration for other specific groups, for example, the unemployed, ethnic minorities.

- the proportion of the total relevant budget which the matter under consideration would involve spending (in order to give a sense of proportion in a situation where this can often be lacking).

- a reminder of the likely proportion of the population of the area which the specific provision might serve.

- a reminder of the authority's equal opportunities policies and how the measure is in accordance with these policies.

Officers may also wish to include statements made by government ministers, as recorded in *Hansard* or in letters, which throw light on the Government's view of how Section 28 will or will not affect specific services and other functions. We have already (see p. 15) discussed the reasons why this is important, particularly before the courts have given a more definitive legal interpretation of Section 28.

Step 3: Is this decision or action prohibited under Section 28?

As the last step in the decision-making process, the local authority must consider whether the action or decision falls foul of Section 28.

Remember that Section 28 prohibits three things:

1. That a local authority shall not intentionally promote homosexuality.

2. That a local authority shall not publish material with the intention of promoting homosexuality.

3. That a local authority shall not promote the teaching in any maintained school of the acceptability of homosexuality as a pretended family relationship.

Section 28

Leaving aside for the time being the third prohibition, which we shall discuss fully in Chapter Four, the local authority would be prudent to ask itself two specific questions in considering whether the decision or action breaches Section 28:

1. Do we intend to promote homosexuality by the proposed decision or action?

What is unusual about Section 28 is that, in contrast to many other limits on the powers of local authorities, in this case what may otherwise be lawful is made unlawful by the *intention* with which it is done. And it is solely the *local authority's intention that is relevant* – not, for example, the intention of the author of a book or other published material.

The intention behind a decision will largely be identified by the statutory power relied upon and those factors taken into account when deciding to exercise a particular statutory power (see steps 1 and 2 above). For example, it could reasonably be inferred that an authority which decides to take a particular course of action in order to counter discrimination against lesbians and gay men intends that it should do just that and no more than that. The significance of the question of intention was illustrated by the Earl of Caithness, the Minister responsible for the Bill in the House of Lords, when he said:

> Local authorities have a duty to provide a comprehensive library service: provided that this and this only, is what they intend to do, there can be no question of the clause inhibiting them from stocking any book that they think necessary for this purpose. Local authorities have power to provide entertainment. Provided that this and this only, is what they are intending to do, there is no reason why the clause should inhibit them from staging plays by Joe Orton or Oscar Wilde.

(If you are not clear about the meaning of 'intention' in Section 28, see Chapter One. For a discussion of how the courts will approach the issue of identifying the local authority's intention, see p. 13.)

2. Even if we do not intend it, is it *highly likely* that the decision or action will in fact 'promote homosexuality'?

Even if a local authority does not intend or desire to 'promote homosexuality', it must consider whether its decision or action is *highly likely* to have this effect; i.e. is highly likely to persuade individuals to become homosexual or to experiment with homosexual relationships which they would not otherwise do.

In this context, it is worth noting that it has been argued that merely the association with the provision of facilities where persons of the same sex might meet would implicate the local authority in the promotion of relationships between them. However, just as it is not a proper function of a public authority to encourage sexual relations of any kind, be they heterosexual or homosexual, it would not be right to deduce from any involvement in the provision of facilities where people may meet an intention to promote sexual relations. (It is not suggested, for example, that the licensing of facilities which are commonly for or used by heterosexuals, or the licensing of sex shops, involves the deliberate promotion of heterosexual relationships between users of those facilities.)

In addition, ministerial statements have made clear that, for example,

> Local authorities have a duty to grant music licences and to consider properly applications for music licences in accordance with the law. I am happy to give the Hon. Gentleman the assurance that, in our understanding of the matter, the clause would not in any way affect the carrying out by local authorities of those duties.
> (*Hansard*, 15.12.87, col. 1020.)

In any event, it is important to remember that a local authority should not be deterred from doing something which is otherwise lawful and desirable merely by the fear that there is a risk that what it does may 'promote homosexuality'. The criterion is whether it is *highly likely* to do so, and merely that there is a risk that it *might* do so would not make the action unlawful.

Summary

In order to ensure that there is no breach of Section 28 and that the local authority is as little open as possible to legal challenge, it is essential that both the officers' report and the resolutions taken in Council clearly and unambiguously identify the following:

- the relevant statutory power authorising what is proposed;
- the relevant factors making the decision reasonable and appropriate and
- the intention of the local authority in making the decision.

Failure to do this might otherwise provide gratuitous opportunities to those who might wish to attack the authority's decision or action. Where a report to Committee is not necessary because an officer is acting under delegated powers, the officer would be well advised to address in written form the same matters which a report would address.

Section 28

Restrictions on local authority publicity

a) The Code of Recommended Practice on Local Authority Publicity

As part of the Government's restrictions on local authority publicity generally, local authorities are now statutorily obliged to consider the **Code of Recommended Practice on Local Authority Publicity (Circular 20/88)**, which came into force on 15 August 1988. This was provided for by Section 4 of the Local Government Act (as amended by Section 27 of the Local Government Act 1988). The Code deals with the content, style, distribution and cost of local authority publicity.

Paragraph 17 of the Code states:

> Publicity should not attack, nor appear to undermine, generally accepted moral standards.

Attention has been drawn to this paragraph in the context of the debates around Section 28. Does the Code have implications for local authorities' activities in relation to homosexual issues?

In legal terms, it is very difficult to see how 'accepted moral standards' can be defined with any certainty. In a recent case (**Stephens v. Avery**, 3 June 1988) it was alleged that the defendant had communicated information about the plaintiff's lesbian relationship to a newspaper in breach of the duty of confidence which she owed her as the recipient of information confidentially given in the context of a personal friendship. Against this it was argued, in part, that no such duty of confidence could exist where the information concerned immoral conduct. But the Vice-Chancellor, Sir Nicholas Browne-Wilkinson, in finding for the plaintiff, said:

> But at the present day no such general code [of sexual morals] exists. There is no common view that sexual conduct of any kind between consenting adults is grossly immoral.

and went on to state further that:

> If it is right that there is now no generally accepted code of sexual morality applying to this case, it would be quite wrong in my judgement for any judge to apply his own personal moral views, however strongly held, in deciding the legal rights of the parties. The court's function is to apply the law, not personal prejudice. Only in a case where there is still a generally accepted moral code can the court refuse to enforce rights in such a way as to offend that generally accepted code.

It is clear from this that, in terms of the law, there is room for a number of sustainable views about what are or are not 'acceptable moral standards'.

It is also important to note that the Code specifically states that it is not intended to 'prohibit the publication of information on politically sensitive or controversial issues, nor stifle public debate' (Paragraph 4 of the Introduction).

The status of the Code was explained by the Minister for the Environment, Christopher Chope MP, in this way:

> The Code is not a series of rules and regulations to which local authorities must adhere in all cases. On the contrary, the Code sets out principles of good practice to act as a benchmark against which authorities must judge their publicity proposals. In each case they will need to consider whether the publicity that they propose to issue is in keeping with the principles set out in the Code. If it is not, they will need to consider whether special circumstances exist which justify departure from the Code.
> (*Hansard*, House of Commons 20.7.88, col. 620.)

Paragraphs 8 and 43 of the Code explain that it will not affect the ability of local authorities to assist voluntary organisations which need to issue publicity as part of their work. However, local authorities are required to *take account* of the Code when giving assistance to such organisations.

In this respect, it has been suggested that it is advisable for local authorities:

- to incorporate the relevant principles of the Code into any published guidance for applicants for grants,

- to make observance of the principles a condition of the grant,

- to monitor the observance of the principles.

However, as Christopher Chope said:

> The extent to which any such monitoring is necessary must remain a matter for the local authority concerned. But in the Government's view prior vetting of all publicity by assisted voluntary organisations would be unnecessary.

b) Section 2 of the Local Government Act 1986

Perhaps not as directly relevant in the context of Section 28 but nevertheless important to note is Section 2 of the Local Government Act 1986 (also amended by Section 27 of the Local Government Act 1988). Section 2 prohibits local authorities from publishing material 'which, in whole or in part, appears to be designed to affect public support for a political party'. The material to be covered is 'any communication, in whatever form, addressed to the public' which will include such things as badges, balloons, stickers, speeches, plays and so on. However, it is important to remember – as with the Code of Practice mentioned above – that such material will not be illegal *simply* because it deals with a question of political controversy.

Nonetheless, Section 2 has in one case been applied to the campaign against Section 28. A video, 'Get your Clause off our lives', was booked to be shown in Wolverhampton's Lighthouse Media Centre, a venue directly funded by the local authority. After invitations had been sent out, the showing was abruptly cancelled on the orders of the Director of Leisure Services, who feared that both the invitation and the video itself could place the local authority in breach of Section 2 of the 1986 Local Government Act. **However, it is difficult to see how this interpretation could actually be substantiated in law.**

A fuller discussion of these restrictions on local authority publicity is contained in *Publish and Still Don't be Damned* (NCVO, 1989).

Chapter Three
Implications for voluntary organisations

People who define themselves as lesbian or gay, like the rest of the population, may make use of the services offered by all kinds of voluntary organisations. Charities, community projects and campaign/pressure groups (such as the National Council for Civil Liberties) all come under the heading of 'voluntary organisations', a term covering a wide range of non-statutory organisations independently managed by voluntary management committees.

Some voluntary organisations have been set up by gay people themselves to address specific needs, and these have led the way in combating discrimination and in developing information networks, support and counselling services for gay people. But many more general voluntary organisations, which are not concerned specifically with lesbian and gay issues, are beginning to examine how their own services can also be made relevant and accessible to lesbians and gay men. This has been in response both to demands from lesbian and gay groups and because of the generally increasing emphasis on the need for equality of opportunity. For example, in 1987 the National Association of Citizens' Advice Bureaux adopted a resolution at its national conference emphasising its commitment to making services relevant to lesbians and gay men.

Local authority support for voluntary groups

Voluntary organisations receive funding from a range of sources – from central government, from charitable trusts, through business sponsorship, from individual donations and from local authorities.

Local authorities have a wide range of funding powers available to them, and these enable them to give grant aid to voluntary organisations for a variety of purposes. The main powers are set out on pp. 24-26. For a more detailed description of these powers see *Getting in on the Act: A Guide to Local Authorities' Powers to Fund Voluntary Organisations* (NCVO,1987).

Local authorities also provide support and facilities to the voluntary sector in other ways; for example, they give access to and allow use of local authority owned equipment, and hire out their venues for events and meetings. Local authorities may also donate the professional expertise of their staff to the voluntary sector – for example, a voluntary group pursuing new premises may have the assistance of local authority architects on the structure and layout of the building.

How, then, will Section 28 affect voluntary organisations?

Section 28 is directed at local authorities and proscribes what they may not do. **It is not directed at voluntary organisations.** It is clear, however, that it will have important implications for these groups, particularly insofar as they receive local authority funding. Section 28 makes it illegal for a local authority to grant-aid (i.e. give public money to) a voluntary organisation if this amounts to intentionally 'promoting homosexuality'.

There are two basic points to be borne in mind here. **First, Section 28 *only* relates to that part of the work of a voluntary group which is funded by the local authority**. Therefore, even if a voluntary group is in *part* grant-aided by a local authority, any activities which are carried out with funds received from other sources do not fall within the remit of Section 28 (provided that a distinction between the use of funds from different funding sources is rigorously maintained by the voluntary organisation).

Second, even if a voluntary group were to 'promote homosexuality' in terms of Section 28 (as interpreted on p. 12), it would not be breaking the law since the law is not directed at voluntary groups. However, as we shall see, local authorities are likely to take steps to ensure that grant-aided voluntary organisations do not place them in a potentially illegal position.

Legal Opinions

It is clear from the legal Opinions obtained that the 'promotion of homosexuality' should not be confused or equated with discouraging forms of discrimination against lesbians and gay men on the ground of their sexuality. It is equally clear that 'welfare' work specifically aimed at lesbians and gay men is not prohibited by the Section.

These legal Opinions reinforce the assurances given by Government spokespeople during parliamentary debates that **voluntary organisations should not in practice have their funding jeopardised by Section 28.**

The activities of voluntary organisations would have to be aimed at persuading people to become homosexual who otherwise would not, perhaps by putting forward homosexuality as preferable to heterosexuality, in order to be promoting homosexuality in the sense defined in the legal Opinions obtained, and there is no evidence that this is in fact what they do. Recently the National Council for Voluntary Organisations (NCVO) examined the activities of a range of organisations providing services for lesbians and gay men and concluded:

> Voluntary organisations do not encourage people to become homosexual or claim that homosexuality is superior to heterosexuality. Instead they aim to offer non-judgemental help and support to people.
> (*Local Government Bill, Clause 28: The Voluntary Sector Perspective*, NCVO, January 1988.)

It does appear that most, if not all, of the kinds of activities carried out by voluntary organisations to provide services and support for lesbians and gay men can continue to be both grant-aided and given other support by local authorities.

In the House of Lords, Government Minister the Earl of Caithness specifically referred to the concern which had been expressed to him about the funding of services provided to lesbians and gay men:

> The National Council for Voluntary Organisations has written to me and no doubt to other noble Lords, suggesting that this clause will prevent the funding in the future of a number of groups offering services to homosexuals. I can reassure it that there is no reason why this should be the case provided that the intention of the local authority is to provide or support a service and the funding is within their powers ... An authority might, for example, wish to finance a voluntary organisation providing counselling and advice services to homosexuals: it is entitled to contribute to the funds of non-profit-making bodies providing a public service – under Section 137(3) of the Local Government Act – if it thinks it appropriate to do so.
> (*Hansard*, 16.2.88, col. 642.)

Excessive caution

It therefore appears that the greatest threat to voluntary sector funding comes not from the terms of Section 28 itself so much as from an *over-cautious* approach to the interpretation of the new law both by local authorities and by voluntary groups themselves. Both may overreact to the Section: local authorities may be concerned about a legal challenge, and voluntary organisations may curtail their services to gay people because they are worried that their overall funding may be under threat.

Voluntary organisations should be aware that some local authorities are now likely to exercise particular caution in deciding whether or not to award a grant for work that is targeted towards the lesbian and gay communities. They may seek to examine in detail areas such as:

- the aims and objectives of the organisation

- its past and current activities and management and its programme for the future

- the specific aims of the project to be funded

- which groups of people are to be targeted

- which sorts of discrimination are being addressed.

In doing this, the local authority will be addressing directly the question of whether the project is likely to 'promote homosexuality' within the meaning of Section 28 outlined in Chapter One (see p. 12).

Local authorities will also be aware that in any possible legal challenge, the **officers' report** on which the funding decision is made by councillors will play an important part, and local authorities are therefore likely to require officers' reports to address these questions in some detail. If you have not already read pp. 23-29 about the preparation of officers' reports, you should now do so.

In addition, the local authority may insist on *careful monitoring* of the funded organisation's activities and in particular of the specific use which it makes of the grant-aid.

Encouraging good practice

Clearly, regardless of Section 28, it is right and proper. that funding decisions of local authorities should be based on full and accurate information, that reasonable monitoring should take place and that voluntary organisations should be accountable to their funding bodies for their use of public funds. This principle has been widely accepted as being in the interests of local authorities and voluntary organisations alike.

However, it is important that such procedures are seen in the context of good practice generally and are negotiated and agreed by local authorities with their local voluntary sector as a whole – and that funding for work with lesbians and gay men is not singled out for unnecessarily severe scrutiny. Over-intensive scrutiny of an organisation could undermine its confidence and its work, and make it difficult for it to achieve its legitimate aims. Remember that, as Michael Barnes QC emphasises in his Opinion, a local authority need not be deterred from doing anything which it is otherwise lawful and desirable that it should do merely by the fear that there is a *slight risk* that what it is doing may have the consequence of 'promoting homosexuality'. This consequence has to be *highly likely* for there to be a problem.

It is in the interest both of the local authority and of voluntary organisations that all these issues are dealt with clearly and unambiguously. **Voluntary groups should ask to see and comment upon the officers' reports before they go to Committee.** If this is not permitted, a proper appeals procedure for refused funding applications becomes essential.

Grant conditions

There is concern that local authorities will impose new grant conditions in order to provide safeguards for the funding body. For example, the London Boroughs Grant Scheme (LBGS), which funds many London-wide voluntary organisations, has introduced a standard condition which reads:

> Grant money may not be expended for any purpose which constitutes the intentional promotion of homosexuality, within the meaning of Section 2A [Section 28] of the Local Government Act 1986.

However, Lord Gifford QC, in his legal Opinion, advises that:

> It is not necessary for local authorities in giving funds to organisations to insert a condition that the organisation should not promote homosexuality. Given the uncertainty of the meaning of these words, such a condition would give rise to considerable confusion. It is the duty of local authorities to satisfy themselves that they, through giving funds to organisations, are not promoting homosexuality. The way to do that is to ensure that officers, in making reports on those organisations, have carried out appropriate checks and have advised members of the non-promotional character of the organisation's work.

If the local authority does wish to include such a condition as a safeguard against a challenge, this could in some circumstances increase the likelihood of groups receiving funding; in other circumstances it could result in an over-cautious approach by officers. Voluntary groups will have to decide for themselves, in the light of local circumstances, whether to contest the imposition of such a grant condition or not.

What should a voluntary organisation do if funding is refused?

If grant-aid is refused, it is important to press the local authority to provide clear reasons in writing for its decision. Only by scrutinising the reasons for the decision will it become apparent whether a local authority is accurately interpreting Section 28.

It may well be that a local authority will claim to be refusing funding for other reasons – for example, the poor performance of the organisation concerned – although its primary motivation is in fact fear of a legal challenge under Section 28.

Although establishing this may be difficult, if a voluntary organisation suspects that this is what has happened, it should:

- attempt to convince the local authority that its fears are groundless, using the information contained in this book.

- seek specialist assistance, particularly legal advice (see p. 64). It may be that the local authority could, and should, be challenged through the courts on its interpretation of Section 28 (see Chapter Five).

- decide not to accept any restrictions and seek alternative funding.

Self-censorship

It is equally important that voluntary organisations themselves resist an over-cautious approach to their work with lesbians and gay men. For example, local authorities may put pressure on voluntary organisations to change their stated aims and objectives or to place increasing emphasis on one aspect of work – for example HIV/AIDS related work – because they see it as less likely to fall foul of the Section.

However, both groups and local authorities should be aware that what they may see as a pragmatic solution dovetails neatly with the view taken by some that, for example, the only legitimate area of voluntary sector work relevant to gay men is that to do with HIV/AIDS. This of course, strengthens the myth that AIDS is a gay problem, a misconception which is extremely dangerous in public health terms and one which all health agencies are strenuously engaged in efforts to correct. It also, by implication, suggests that gay equals AIDS, and denies the range of oppression and discrimination experienced by lesbians and gay men, distorts the other services voluntary groups may seek to provide to combat this, and undermines the independence of voluntary organisations.

If presented with a requirement for changes in its stated aims and objectives, a voluntary organisation will need to consider carefully whether the changes are in fact necessary, and whether accepting them will be best for the organisation and the community it serves.

In practice, far from displaying excessive caution in the face of Section 28, over 350 London voluntary organisations have signed a declaration deploring the introduction of the new law, declaring their commitment to continuing and developing services to lesbians and gay men and to advancing equal opportunities generally. Indeed, instead of deterring voluntary organisations from providing services, Section 28 *could* provide a major impetus for many voluntary organisations who work with the public at large to re-examine the extent to which they have created conditions in which their services are relevant and accessible to lesbians and gay men, with a view to improving and expanding the quality of service in the future.

Recent funding decisions

There have been a series of funding decisions since Section 28 became law. The London Boroughs Grants Scheme, which was set up following the abolition of the Greater London Council to fund voluntary groups across London, has funded the following organisations since May 1988:

- *Black Lesbian and Gay Centre Project*
  provides training, information, advice and counselling

- *Friend*
  provides counselling, advice, information and organises social events

- *Lesbian Archive*
  an archive collection of publications, documents, films and music

- *Lesbian and Gay Employment Rights*
  fights employment discrimination against lesbians and gay men

- *London Lesbian and Gay Centre*
  offers a broad range of activities, both educational and social

- *London Lesbian Line*
  provides information, advice and counselling by telephone

- *GALOP* (Gay and Lesbian Policing Group)
  provides advice and information to lesbians and gay men dealing with the police and the law and as victims of violence

- *Gay Bereavement Project*
  provides counselling for bereaved lesbians and gay men

- *GLLAD* (Gay and Lesbian Legal Advice) legal advice by telephone

- *London Lesbian and Gay Switchboard* 24-hour telephone information service on a range of matters including HIV/AIDS

The above descriptions are taken from the 'Review of London's Needs 87/88' report prepared for the London Boroughs Grants Scheme by the London Research Centre.

Grants to the above organisations totalled £295,000 for 1988-89.

Other organisations provide specific services to lesbians and gay men but are not listed because they did not apply for grants as lesbian or gay organisations.

Chapter Four

Implications for education

Education was a key issue in the debates over the Section, both inside and outside Parliament. The supporters of the Section placed great emphasis upon various 'scare' stories published in the popular press, which purported to describe current educational practice in some London boroughs. For example, there was a widespread and persistent story that two-year-olds attending play centres in Lambeth had been 'exposed' to gay and lesbian books. This story, which originated in an article in the *Evening Standard* in November 1987, was never substantiated – but it became part of the folklore surrounding the alleged activities of the 'loony left' and was repeated frequently in the parliamentary debate over the Section.

At best, such stories were wild distortions, while several were exposed as complete fabrications; and despite repeated challenges to do so, the supporters of the Section were never able to name a single school in which the kind of 'gay lesson' they claimed to find so objectionable had actually taken place.

What does happen in schools, however, is the bullying of children because they – or their parents – are believed to be gay. Teenagers who are becoming aware of their sexuality often suffer in terrified isolation and according to the report which the London Gay Teenage Group commissioned in 1984, 60 per cent of them in London have suffered harassment at school and 20 per cent have attempted or seriously considered suicide. As one gay parent wrote to The *Guardian* (10 February 1988) during the parliamentary debate:

> I have a 3½-year-old daughter. She lives with myself and the woman with whom I have lived for 15 years. We have a wide circle of friends and relations who totally accept her circumstances ... Soon she will be starting primary school. We are aware that as she grows older she will have to deal with anti-homosexual prejudice. We had hoped that if such prejudice is expressed by her peers at school her teachers would be in a position to challenge it and perhaps even to create an atmosphere of greater tolerance and understanding within the school ... [Clause 28] will be a licence for bigots to torment a child because her parents are 'queer'. I believe my child has as much right as any other to have her home and family respected and not to be tormented or harassed because of her family circumstances. I hope that in coming to their decisions on the proposed legislation, the members of both Houses of Parliament will think about what is actually going to become of children such as mine (and there are many of them), and what kind of bigoted and vengeful world they are creating for her to live in.

Section 28

Haringey Council in North London had tried to take such issues on board in November 1985, when their Education Committee adopted an Equal Opportunities Policy Statement for employment and service delivery. A twenty-seven member Curriculum Working Party was assigned to review guidelines for handling lesbian and gay issues in schools. It included four head teachers, three deputy heads, other senior teachers, an adviser and professional assistant from the education service, and members of the Council's Lesbian and Gay Unit.

But before the committee had even assembled for its first meeting, opposition developed into the formation of the Parents' Rights Group, which received wide media coverage for its inaccurate claims that the Council was proposing lessons in lesbian and gay sexual practices for children in all schools in Haringey.

Section 28 does not, in law, prevent local education authorities adopting an equal opportunities policy which pledges action to end discrimination against lesbian and gay people. But both education authorities and education professionals cannot but be aware that their handling of issues relating to homosexuality will now come under close and often deliberately obstructive scrutiny. **How, then, ought LEAs and teachers to conduct themselves with due regard to their overall legal obligations as well as to their professional ones?**

There are complex issues of duty and liability here, and so this chapter will examine the following questions in turn:

- How does Section 28 fit with the existing legislation on education?
- What does Section 28 prohibit education authorities from doing?
- How does Section 28 affect the content of teaching?
- How does Section 28 affect teachers as employees and LEAs as employers?
- How does Section 28 affect LEAs as providers of other educational services?

From a legal point of view, it is important to stress that **existing education legislation continues to apply and forms the context within which Section 28 must be seen.**

How does Section 28 fit with the existing legislation on education?

The duty of equal treatment

As we have seen (Chapter One, p. 10) local authorities have a duty not to discriminate in the way they exercise their functions between one individual and another. The duty of equal treatment and the obligation not to discriminate applies to local authorities in their educational functions as in all their other functions.

In relation to its employees: an LEA continues to have the normal responsibilities of a good employer, and these include an obligation to ensure that employees are not subject to discrimination or victimisation because of matters unrelated to the performance of their work. Far too often, examples of ill-informed prejudice towards, and victimisation of, lesbian and gay teachers occur. **Local authorities continue to have a duty to confront such prejudice and to improve their own employment practice where necessary.**

The Earl of Caithness (the Government Minister responsible for the Bill in the House of Lords) said:

> Noble Lords have not raised the point but the clause is not about banning the employment of homosexuals by local authorities. Like all public bodies, local authorities should be, and I'm sure are, equal opportunity employers.

The Government's professed intention with regard to discrimination was emphasised by the Earl of Caithness in the House of Lords:

> Let me make it absolutely clear at the outset that the clause in no way imposes some form of discrimination against homosexuals. The Government are firmly opposed to all forms of discrimination.

In relation to school pupils and to students in further education: this duty of 'equal treatment' is emphasised by provisions in the **1944 Education Act**. For example, **Section 7** of the **1944 Act** places a duty on local education authorities

> to contribute towards the spiritual, moral, mental and physical development of the community by securing that sufficient education throughout those stages (i.e. primary, secondary and further education) shall be available to meet the needs of the population of their area.

The need to take account of the particular characteristics of *every* pupil is underlined in **Section 8**, which lays down that schools must be sufficient in character:

to afford for all pupils opportunities for education offering such variety of instruction and training as may be desirable in view of their different ages, abilities and aptitudes ...

If Section 28 is viewed in the general context of existing education laws and in terms of accepted good professional practice, then at a basic level, **local education authorities and teachers continue to have a duty to promote and protect the welfare of each individual pupil irrespective of how the pupil comes to define her or his own sexuality and whether or not she or he is part of a family which includes a homosexual relationship.** Section 28 should not be interpreted in any way which conflicts with this duty, or which disregards the existence and needs of children who identify as gay or lesbian, or who live in families which include such a relationship.

What does Section 28 prohibit education authorities from doing?

Section 28 introduces three prohibitions on local authorities (which include local education authorities). It prohibits them from:

- intentionally promoting homosexuality.

- publishing material with the intention of promoting homosexuality.

- promoting the teaching in any maintained school of the acceptability of homosexuality as a pretended family relationship.

Because it is only the third prohibition which *specifically* refers to what may not be promoted in maintained schools, some have concluded that this is the only prohibition to which LEA action in these schools is subject. *In fact, all three prohibitions apply to the functions of LEAs in schools and elsewhere.* But because the third prohibition refers specifically to schools, it does not apply to further education and other non-school activities of the LEA, where the authority's role is governed only by the first two prohibitions. (For further discussion of the legal interpretation of the three prohibitions, see Chapter One, p. 11. For a definition of 'maintained schools' see subsection (4) of Section 28 in Appendix One p.65)

It must be emphasised that the prohibitions are directed at the activities of local education authorities. **Section 28 is not aimed at school governors or teachers and nothing that they do or may do is made illegal by it, although there may be other implications for these groups which are discussed on p. 52.**

So, under the first two prohibitions of Section 28, LEAs are now under a duty to ensure that, in the making of their policy on their schools' curricula, both on sex education and other matters, and including the provision of classroom aids and materials, they do not 'intentionally promote homosexuality'. What does this mean?

As we have seen, Lord Gifford, in his legal Opinion on the particular implications of Section 28 for education, concludes that:

> to 'promote homosexuality' involves active advocacy directed by local authorities towards individuals in order to persuade them to become homosexual or to experiment with homosexual relationships who otherwise would not. (For a fuller discussion of this, see p. 12.)

How Section 28 affects the non-school education activities of LEAs is discussed later, on p. 53. For the time being, it should be noted that the local authorities' role in deciding what is taught in sex education is relatively limited, so that even in the unlikely event that a local authority wished to persuade individuals to become homosexual, it would not in fact have the power to impose this policy on its schools. If, however, a local authority wishes to adopt a policy which *advises* that the school curriculum should include consideration of the issue of gay and lesbian sexuality (as both a political issue in relation to equal opportunities and as part of an explanation of different forms of sexuality in sex education) Section 28 would *not* prohibit it from doing so. The reasons why are discussed more fully below.

How does Section 28 affect the content of teaching?

Existing laws on sex education

Section 46 of the **Education (No.2) Act 1986** requires LEAs, governing bodies and head teachers to:

> take such steps as are reasonably practicable to secure that where sex education is given to any registered pupils of the school it is to be given in such a manner as to encourage those pupils to have due regard to moral considerations and the value of family life.

Although no guidance has been given on the concept of 'the value of family life', it is reasonable to assume that it refers to the importance of healthy and loving family relationships between both the child and her or his close household, and those between the future adult and her or his partner and children. In present day society such words must denote a broad view of the family and one which is not limited to married life.

Under the Education (No.2) Act 1986, LEAs have a duty to determine and keep under review their policy in relation to the secular curriculum of maintained schools. Except in the case of sex education, it is the duty of the head teacher to ensure that the school's curriculum is compatible with LEA policy. **In relation to sex education, the governing body of the school has the final voice.**

It is the duty of the governing body to consider whether sex education should form part of the secular curriculum and to make a separate written statement of its policy. The LEA may therefore propose a policy with regard to sex education but if the governors do not agree with it, it is their view which prevails.

The LEA cannot normally intervene if it disagrees. However, if the policy adopted by the governors is considered by the local education authority to be wholly unreasonable and not in the best interest of the pupils, it could make a complaint to the Secretary of State for Education and Science. It is also possible for a local education authority to institute proceedings for a Judicial Review of the governors' decision (see Chapter Five, Legal Challenges).

If the governors' policy on sex education is incompatible with any part of the syllabus for a course which leads to a public examination, however, the law states that it is to be disregarded.

Government circulars relating to sex education

Further clarification is given by government circulars relating to education. These do not in themselves have the force of law, but they are usually issued when the department concerned wishes to give guidance on the application of a new law or wishes to communicate policy statements, and where they contain legal advice the courts will take notice of this. Whether a local authority follows or does not follow the advice given in a circular may therefore be of evidential value in a case, and for this reason LEAs, school governors and head teachers alike should consider circulars carefully. Where they decide against the advice given in a circular, they should record the reasons why they have done so. (See p. 15 for more on the legal status of government statements and circulars.)

In the particular case of sex education, there are two statements in **Circular 11/87** of the Department of Education and Science which are worth noting:

21.   Schools cannot, in general, avoid tackling controversial sexual matters, such as contraception and abortion, by reason of their sensitivity. Pupils may well ask questions about them and schools should be prepared to offer balanced and factual information and to acknowledge the major ethical issues involved.

However,

22.   There is no place in any school in any circumstances for teaching which advocates homosexual behaviour, which presents it as 'the norm', or which encourages homosexual experimentation by pupils.

This means that there is a clear recognition that balanced and factual (but not proselytising) teaching about homosexuality may, and indeed should, form part of the sex education syllabus in schools.

This is in line with previous guidance issued by the DES. For example, *Health Education from 5 to 16* HMSO (1986), published in the series 'Curriculum Matters' by H.M. Inspectors, says:

> Given the openness with which homosexuality is treated in society now it is almost bound to arise as an issue in one area or another of a school's curriculum. Information about and discussion of homosexuality, whether it involves a whole class or an individual, needs to acknowledge that experiencing strong feelings of attraction to members of the same sex is a phase passed through by many young people, but that for a significant number of people these feelings persist into adult life. Therefore it needs to be dealt with objectively and seriously, bearing in mind that, while there has been a marked shift away from the general condemnation of homosexuality, many individuals and groups within society hold sincerely to the view that it is morally objectionable. This is difficult territory for teachers to traverse, and for some schools to accept that homosexuality may be a normal feature of relationships would be a breach of the religious faith upon which they are founded. Consequently, LEAs, voluntary bodies, governors, heads and senior staff in schools have important responsibilities in devising guidance and supporting teachers dealing with this sensitive issue.

It can therefore be argued that Parliament must have been aware of the continuing Government position on the treatment of homosexuality in schools, and did not intend that Section 28 should conflict radically with it. In fact, **Circular 12/88**, the most recent circular from the Department of Environment, which was published as Section 28 came into force, confirms this view. The relevant section states:

> Section 28 does not affect the activities of school governors, nor of teachers. It will not prevent the objective discussion of homosexuality in the classroom, nor the counselling of pupils concerned about their sexuality. Such activities will continue to be governed by Section 46 of the Education (No.2) Act 1986. Guidance on this and on government

policy on sex education at school, is provided in DES Circular 11/87...
(See Appendix Three, p. 73 for the full text of Circular 12/88.)

Section 28's prohibition on teaching the acceptability of homosexuality as a 'pretended family relationship'

It is worth remembering that Section 28 had its origins in the Bill drafted by Lord Halsbury in 1986 which focused specifically on the issue of the promotion of homosexuality as an 'acceptable family relationship' both in and out of schools. At that time, the Government's view was that the Bill was unnecessary, because changes in education law meant that LEAs no longer had direct role in determining the kind of sex education taught in schools. The Government also expressed reservations about how such a prohibition might be interpreted in practice.

Why then, did the Government do an effective U-turn when the clause made its second appearance in the Local Government Bill (1987), insisting at that point on the inclusion of the third prohibition (concerning homosexuality as a family relationship), when it could be argued that the issue is already covered in the general prohibitions against promoting homosexuality? The Earl of Caithness, on behalf of the Government, explained this decision as follows:

> We think it is right to make it clear on the face of the legislation that local authorities should not be using their limited powers to encourage teaching that portrays homosexual relationships which have the appearance of being family relationships, in most senses of that phrase, as being on those grounds *a welcome development or one to be emulated.*

And further, that

> The purpose of the phrase 'teaching ... the acceptability of homosexuality as a pretended family relationship' is to indicate that the local authorities should not be using their powers under Section 17 of the Education (No. 2) Act 1986 to encourage the teaching that relationships between two people of the same sex can and do *play the same role in society as the traditional family.*
> (In both quotations, the emphasis is ours.)

The crux of the matter, then, appears to be the Government's objection to the idea that homosexual relationships might have the same standing in society as heterosexual family relationships. The word 'pretended' adds little to the sense, but appears to underline Parliament's view that a homosexual family relationship is not a 'real' family relationship.

As Michael Howard QC, MP, put it, for the Government, in the House of Commons:

> ... the precise purpose of the new Section 2A [Section 28] was to put into legislative form the principle set out in the recent Department of Education and Science Circular on sex education that homosexuality should not be portrayed as the norm. It is not right for pupils to be taught, in any school, that it is the norm. It is even less acceptable for local authorities to promote such teaching.

Remembering that the prohibition is directed not at teachers but at local authorities and that local authorities have little power to promote the content of sex education in schools, it would appear that the kind of activity this part of the Section is intended to prohibit is, for example, any recommendation by LEAs that schools should have in their libraries books like *Jenny Lives with Eric and Martin*, the picture book referred to in the Introduction, which describes the unremarkable daily life of a little girl who lives with her gay father and his partner.

In ILEA, one copy of *Jenny Lives with Eric and Martin* was available in a teachers' centre as a resource which teachers could consult when counselling a pupil with homosexual parents. The ILEA's Chief Education Officer had in fact ruled that it *not* be made available in school libraries. **The third prohibition of Section 28 does not prevent an LEA including books which represent homosexual families as of equal standing in society as heterosexual families on resource lists for the use of teachers themselves, or in teachers' centres for use when counselling pupils.** It would probably, however, prohibit an LEA advocating, through a resource list or otherwise, that such material be used generally in the classroom or be freely available in a school library.

Nor does the third prohibition of Section 28 alter the duty of teachers towards the welfare of their pupils. For example, in relation to the counselling of individual pupils, the Earl of Caithness maintained that, notwithstanding the prohibition on teaching that portrays homosexual relationships as 'a welcomed development or one to be emulated',

> We believe that the wording of paragraph 2A expressed this mischief well, that it in no way prevents local authorities from advocating a tolerant and non-discriminatory approach to children living in such relationships and that it in no way interferes with the proper role of teachers.

Section 28

He emphasised that:

> The paragraph is directed solely at local authorities, not at the teachers. The local authority's only function in this field is now to state its views in a statement under Section 17 of the Education (No. 2) Act 1986. As I have explained, the governing body is not bound by that statement. The teacher is answerable to the governing body and not to the local authority.

There was concern, expressed by Lord Gifford in the House of Lords, that an implication of the Section would be that it would become difficult for a teacher, faced with a pupil being bullied because she or he lived with homosexual parents, to say: 'Don't worry. Your parents' relationship is one of many kinds of relationship in the world. There is nothing wrong with it. It is just different from other people's and you should not be bullied because of it.' In fact the statements above make it clear that the Government does *not* intend such counselling from a teacher to be in breach of Section 28. A teacher would be entitled to support the child by affirming that such a family is acceptable and would also be entitled to raise the issue in the class generally, both on account of the welfare of the individual pupil and also in an attempt to combat prejudice.

It should also be noted that there is no legal definition of 'family' which excludes lesbians and gay men. Nothing in Section 28 affects the definition of 'parent' in the Education Act 1944 Section 114 as including, in addition to natural and legal parents, 'a guardian and every person who has the actual custody of the child or young person'. Whether or not that definition includes the partner of a natural parent, either heterosexual or homosexual, depends on the actual circumstances of the individual household.

Homosexuality in contexts other than sex education

Although it is most likely that homosexuality will be discussed in the context of personal development and as part of the sex education curriculum, the issue may also be discussed in a number of different contexts. For older children, the issue could be discussed in relation to different attitudes to homosexuality in society past and present and may therefore be raised in English, History, the Social Sciences or within an arts programme.

It has been feared that teachers might be restricted in the range of texts they may choose as a result of Section 28. Government statements have made clear that it was *not* intended that Section 28 should have that effect: teachers remain free to discuss, for example, the homoerotic content in Shakespeare's sonnets, in the love poems of Auden, in Lawrence's *Rainbow* or in Virginia Woolf's *Mrs Dalloway* – all books which have been used as school texts in the past.

Further education

The position of teachers and lecturers in further education establishments is similar to that of teachers in schools: Section 28 is not directed at them and nothing that they may do is made illegal by it. As in schools, Section 28 does not prohibit a balanced and factual discussion of homosexual issues in further education teaching, nor does it restrict the pastoral role of teachers in relation to their students.

It is the LEA which may not intentionally promote homosexuality or publish material which promotes homosexuality in further education establishments, and insofar as the LEA has responsibility for deciding or advising on courses, and for supplying teaching materials, it is bound by the *first two prohibitions* contained in Section 28. The third prohibition relating to the promotion of the teaching of the acceptability of homosexuality as a pretended family relationship applies only to maintained schools and *not* to further education establishments.

With the forthcoming reorganisation of further education under the Education Reform Act 1988, the role of LEAs in further education will greatly diminish. The proposed governing bodies which will run further education establishments will not be bound by Section 28.

In summary, nothing in Section 28 prohibits any teacher from dealing with the subject of homosexuality in an honest and objective way with pupils in the classroom. This has been made clear both in government statements on Section 28 and in the relevant circulars. Teachers are under a general duty to consider and protect the welfare of their pupils. Nothing in Section 28 requires them to act in a way contrary to this duty.

For example, teachers retain the freedom to counsel individual pupils about their sexuality. Pastoral counselling in school should include the same respect for a young person's welfare and well-being whether they are gay or heterosexual. Likewise, teachers will continue to be involved in protecting pupils from bullying and victimisation from other children who may taunt them because they, or their parents, are believed to be gay. To deal with such a situation by reassuring the pupil, and by giving an honest and factual explanation of homosexual relationships to the other pupils, must be part of the general duty of those involved in education to foster and protect the welfare of their pupils. Advertisements which give pupils information about help and counselling services are also not affected. A notice about Gayline is as acceptable as one for the Brook Advisory Centre.

Section 28

How does Section 28 affect teachers as employees and LEAs as employers?

Until the Education Reform Act 1988 comes into force, teachers in further education might face disciplinary proceedings by their employing authority if it were to be considered that they had taken action likely to bring the authority into contravention of the Section. In schools, too, under **Section 41** of the **Education (No.2) Act 1986**, LEAs have the power to investigate complaints about teachers and to take disciplinary action against them, including dismissal. This is subject to various requirements for consultation with the governing body and the head teacher.

At the time of writing, the governing body of a school has the power to recommend to the LEA that a person should cease to work at that school. The LEA is bound to consider their recommendation, but is not required to accept it. However, it should be noted that this position will be radically altered when the **Education Reform Act 1988** comes into effect. Under **Section 37** of this Act, all powers of appointment and dismissal of schools which have a delegated budget will pass to the governors.

The Gifford Opinion considers that Section 28 does have a bearing on the current powers of LEAs. For example, if a teacher was persistently 'promoting homosexuality' in the sense defined in Chapter One, and was recommended for dismissal by the governors, the LEA would be bound to consider the evidence that the teacher was behaving in this way in making their decision. However, as the legal Opinion states:

> Provided teachers deal with questions of sexuality and prejudice in ways which they believe to be honest and objective, it is difficult to see that disciplinary procedures could be appropriate, still less that the local authority could be in breach of the law.

On the contrary, as the Opinion points out, it could be a breach of law for a local education authority to *overreact* to a complaint about a teacher's conduct and take action which could be harmful to the interests of both the teacher and his or her pupils. As Lord Gifford's Opinion goes on to say:

> Finally, it is important to note that teachers retain the right, indeed the duty, to protect the welfare of their pupils. That will clearly involve teachers in protecting pupils from bullying and victimisation from other children who may taunt them because they or their parents are believed to be lesbian or gay.

Lesbian and gay teachers

In the case of a teacher who is himself gay or herself lesbian, it must be that person's decision as to how they deal with the fact of their sexuality with their pupils. A relationship of honesty and trust between teacher and pupils is an essential ingredient of effective teaching. Questions of a teacher's own sexuality may arise and nothing in the law prevents a teacher from referring to his or her own sexual orientation if that is a natural thing to do in the fostering of such a relationship of trust. There is no reason to believe that lesbian or gay teachers will discuss their sexual activities with pupils any more than a heterosexual teacher would. LEAs should respect any decision to respond to pupils with honesty and openness, and should give their support to teachers who adopt this position; at the very least, they should show themselves most reluctant to intervene in such decisions taken in good faith.

However, LEAs do not always behave in such an enlightened manner, and the National Council for Civil Liberties has in the past advised many teachers who have been the subject of a complaint, an investigation or disciplinary proceedings as a result of what they are alleged to have said in the classroom. While Section 28 was being debated in Parliament, Dr Austin Allen, a maths teacher in a Bradford secondary school, was told that his contract as a supply teacher would not be renewed after he had answered direct questions from pupils about his lifestyle. He was quoted the text of Clause 28 (as it then stood) by the Education Officer in support of this decision. Following opposition from Dr Allen's head teacher, the Chair of the school governors and his union, the NUT, the Labour-controlled city council reversed the decision.

How does Section 28 affect local education authorities as providers of other educational services?

Among their educational services, LEAs:

- provide books in school libraries from central LEA lending facilities
- organise Theatre-in-Education tours of plays
- provide in-service training
- invite outside speakers to their classes
- fund youth work

How might these activities be affected by Section 28? Lord Gifford's legal Opinion is clear that, provided that the LEA does not through any of these activities *intend to promote homosexuality* in the sense defined in Chapter One the simple inclusion of a homosexual theme or the raising of homosexuality as an issue in any of these activities remains perfectly lawful.

A play by the Avon Touring Theatre Company was banned by the head teacher of a school at which it was to be performed because he believed it contravened Section 28. In our view, this was an inaccurate understanding of the law. In East Sussex, the Education Officer ordered that the directory published by the National Youth Bureau (a long-established and respected body), which contains details of over a hundred projects or organisations offering voluntary work opportunities for young people, should not be distributed to schools because it contains a reference to one organisation which asks for gay and lesbian volunteers over the age of 14 'with a positive attitude to their sexuality'. Lord Gifford's legal Opinion is categorical that the view taken by this authority was wrong. To inform young people about gay and lesbian organisations in which they might do voluntary work, or from which they might get advice, can in no way be held to constitute the promotion of homosexuality.

Youth work

In deciding to fund a Gay and Lesbian Teenage Group, the LEA needs to satisfy itself that it is not intending to 'promote homosexuality' in the sense defined in Chapter One. But it is likely that the fundamental objective of the LEA here will be the provision of social education in its broad sense, i.e. aimed at ensuring that young gay and lesbian people, just as much as young heterosexual people, develop their personal resources and equip themselves as responsible members of a free society.

The intention, therefore, will be to enable these young people to make sense of the issues affecting their lives: their sexuality, the prejudice, intolerance and even hatred they face, and the need for equal opportunities, both in the context of their local community and in society in general.

Particular gay and lesbian youth work should be set in the context of comparable provision which is made, for example, for girls and young women, teenagers from ethnic minorities, or young people with disabilities. Intending to encourage sexual acts between young people (whether heterosexual or male homosexual) below the respective ages of consent is, of course, against the law, and it has been suggested that, simply by providing the facility, the local education authority would be implicated in promoting such acts. However, just as it is not a proper function of a public authority to encourage sexual relations of any kind, be they heterosexual or homosexual, it would not be right to deduce from a local authority's involvement in the provision of such facilities an intention to promote sexual relations, which are a matter for the individuals concerned. (This is the principle which applies, for example, to the local authority licensing of sex shops.) However, as Lord Gifford's legal Opinion states, 'Different considerations might arise if an organisation was aggressively going out to recruit members by advertising homosexuality in persuasive terms as a way of life which young people should try out.'

Student Unions

Local education authorities also fund student unions. Some student unions have already had restrictions imposed upon them, or have been warned that they may lose their local authority funding, because they have engaged in activities with which it is alleged the local authority cannot be involved without contravening Section 28. For example, the Director of the City of Leeds College of Music banned the student union's Gay and Lesbian Society from meeting on college premises. In another incident, the Deputy Director of Education at Strathclyde Regional Council wrote to all Colleges of Further Education stating that grants to student associations would be withheld unless they agreed to cease all lesbian and gay related activities. In Essex the County Council issued a directive to principals of FE colleges instructing them to ban lesbian and gay groups from meeting in colleges or in other council-owned buildings.

In none of these cases, according to a specific legal Opinion sought by the National Union of Students and according to the Opinions which form the basis for this book, was such action justified under Section 28. The Essex directive was in fact withdrawn in May 1989, after the NUS threatened legal action.

Any LEA involved in funding a gay and lesbian organisation is bound by exactly the same considerations as apply to the local authority as a whole in funding voluntary organisations in general. These are detailed on pp. 23-29.

For further reading: the Association of London Authorities has produced an alternative circular, *Personal Relationships and Sex Education at School*, which advises on policy and good practice, including issues arising from Section 28. Copies of the circular may be obtained from the ALA at 36 Old Queen Street, London SW1H 9JF.

Mirrors around the walls – Respecting Diversity, the report of Haringey Council's curriculum working party, gives examples of good practice and makes a number of reccommendations, including that its findings be widely discussed in the local community. A copy of the report may be obtained from Haringey Education Service, 48-62 Station Road, London N22 4TY.

Chapter Five
Legal challenges

From the legal Opinions obtained, it would appear that there are few, if any, existing local authority activities which are outlawed by Section 28. Nevertheless, legal challenges must be expected. The challenge may come from those who wish to prevent local authorities from performing certain roles – for example, funding a particular voluntary organisation; or, conversely, from individuals or organisations whose work or activities are impeded by a local authority on the grounds of Section 28.

A local authority can only do that which it has power to do. If it exceeds its powers, it can be challenged in the courts. A local authority which does something prohibited by Section 28 has exceeded its powers and, equally, one which overreacts in fear of Section 28 may do something – for example, sacking a teacher or banning an organisation from its premises – which exceeds its powers.

Breach of Section 28 does not constitute a criminal offence. Neither members nor the officers of a local authority can be prosecuted simply because it is alleged that they have done something prohibited by Section 28.

Judicial Review

Any individual, alone or on behalf of an organisation with a legitimate interest, can initiate action in the High Court to challenge the decision or action of a local authority which they believe to be outside its powers. Very often the person taking such proceedings is a ratepayer, or a number of ratepayers together. These proceedings are called **Judicial Review**, because their aim is to review in the courts the local authority's decision.

An applicant for Judicial Review must first apply for 'leave' of the court. This means they must show the court that there is an arguable case and obtain the court's permission to proceed with it. The application for leave can often be made *ex parte* (i.e. without informing the local authority), so the authority would not necessarily know if an application had been *unsuccessfully* made.

Before the full hearing of the case, the court may make certain interim (temporary) orders. The one most commonly sought is an **injunction** designed to preserve the status quo. In practice, because of the time delays involved, such an injunction could operate to prevent the carrying out of a local authority decision. Even if the authority eventually won, by the time the case was heard the original decision might have been overtaken by events – for example, the community arts festival at which a play was to be performed might already have taken place. If, at the final hearing of the case, the applicant is successful, the court has a wide range of powers. It can order the local authority to pay **damages**, and it can make a range of other orders. In relation to a challenge under Section 28, the most likely court orders are:

- *a certiorari*: quashing the decision of the local authority. The authority would be directed to reconsider its decision in accordance with the court's judgment

- **a prohibition**: restraining the local authority from acting in excess of its powers

- **a declaration**: that the action or decision proposed by the local authority is in breach of Section 28.

Declaration

As an alternative to Judicial Review, there is another procedure under which the High Court can make binding declarations on a point of law even where no other remedy is being sought. This procedure could be used to gain an authoritative legal interpretation of Section 28. However, the courts will not entertain purely academic questions; the case must be about an *actual* local authority decision.

The District Auditor

The District Auditor can apply to the court for a declaration that an item of expenditure is unlawful. The court can order the person or persons responsible (usually the councillors who voted for it) to repay the unlawful expenditure and to be disqualified from holding office for a specified period. Individual ratepayers can also raise matters with the District Auditor when they believe there is unlawful expenditure. It is a defence to actions brought by District Auditors if those responsible for the expenditure acted *reasonably* or *in the belief that the spending was lawful.*

The Local Government Act 1988 also gives the Auditor new powers to *prevent* suspected unlawful expenditure before the spending has actually taken place and without the need to apply to court. The local authority may appeal to the High Court if it disagrees with the Auditor's decision.

Wrongful restriction of powers

One of the main dangers of Section 28, as we have seen, is that some local authorities, fearful of being challenged for exceeding their powers, will refuse to take decisions or carry out actions which are perfectly lawful. Others may use Section 28 simply to justify their refusal to fund certain activities or organisations, or to provide other support or services for lesbians and gay men.

As emphasised in Chapter Three on p. 37, if Section 28 is cited as grounds for refusing, for example, the funding of a particular organisation, the local authority should be pressed to *explain in full* how it is interpreting the Section. It may be possible for an individual or organisation affected by a restrictive interpretation of Section 28 to challenge the local authority by Judicial Review proceedings in the High Court (see above).

Such a challenge would be successful if the court took the view that no reasonable authority properly directing itself in law and taking account of all relevant matters could have made such a decision. However, it should be noted that the courts are generally unlikely to order that a local authority *must* fund an organisation or carry out a particular activity if its powers to do so are discretionary only.

A local authority which insists upon a restrictive interpretation of Section 28 could be challenged by seeking a declaration (see above). This would provide clarification as to whether the local authority's interpretation of Section 28 in relation to the funding or support for an activity is one which would be supported by the courts.

As any such challenge is dealing with a new and complex law, it is essential that specialist legal advice is obtained before any individual or organisation decides to take such action. Organisations which may be contacted for such assistance are listed at the back of this book.

Challenges over educational matters

Section 68 of the Education Act 1944 provides that the Secretary of State may intervene if, either on complaint by any person or otherwise, he is satisfied that an LEA, or the governors of any school,

> have acted or are proposing to act unreasonably with respect to the exercise of any power conferred or the performance of any duty imposed by or under this Act.

There is also provision in **Section 67** of the Act for various disputes between LEAs and the governors of a school to be referred to the Secretary of State for determination. This means that in most cases where governors are thought to be unreasonable in their treatment of homosexual issues in a school the only remedy is by way of complaint to the Minister. **Section 68** effectively precludes the courts from considering such cases. If, on the other hand, a *local authority* is thought to be acting *in breach of Section 28*, rather than merely acting unreasonably, it would be possible for the LEA to be challenged in Judicial Review proceedings on the basis that it was acting in excess of its powers and in breach of law.

Section 28

Breach of the European Convention on Human Rights

Article 8 of the European Convention on Human Rights provides that 'everyone has the right to respect for his private and family life, his home and correspondence'.

In two cases, this Article has been specifically applied by the European Court of Human Rights to protect gay men. In the case of **Dudgeon v United Kingdom (1981)** the court held that legislation which made all sexual acts between men illegal in Northern Ireland violated the Convention. It said:

> The maintenance in force of the impugned legislation constitutes a continuing interference with the applicant's right to respect for his private life (which includes his sexual life) within the meaning of Article 8(1).

Similarly, in the recent case of **Norris v Republic of Ireland (October 1988)**, the court again held that the existence of legislation penalising certain homosexual acts carried out in private between consenting adult males constitutes a breach of Article 8.

In both cases the court rejected the claim that the legislation was justifiable under Article 8(2) for the protection of morals and for the protection of the rights of others.

Such rulings are important because they confirm that under the Convention the sexuality, and indeed the sexual life, of a gay man or lesbian woman requires to be respected. Therefore, any interpretation of Section 28 which required a local authority to show disrespect for homosexual people would cause a conflict with the Convention.

Article 14 of the Convention is also relevant. It provides that the enjoyments and the rights and freedoms set forth in the Convention shall be secured 'without discrimination on any ground such as sex, race, colour ... or other status.' According to Lord Gifford's legal Opinion, Article 14 is wide enough to prevent discrimination against individuals on the ground of their sexual orientation.

A restrictive action or decision under Section 28 could therefore give rise to an application to the European Convention on Human Rights. **As it may be necessary first to exhaust all remedies in the British courts, it is again essential that specialist legal advice is taken before submitting such an application.**

Conclusion

Section 28 is at once more limited and more wide-ranging in its effects than it might at first appear. On the one hand, it is likely to be limited in its strictly *legal* effects, because, as Michael Barnes QC put it in his Opinion, 'It is open to serious doubt whether [Section 28] will render unlawful many decisions or actions presently lawful', and because it is so ill-drafted.

On the other hand, Section 28 symbolises and gives important constitutional legitimacy to greater hostility and intolerance. Bernard Levin, in an article in *The Times*, accurately described it as 'prejudicial, unnecessary, discriminatory and liable to arouse hatred' and it would indeed be naïve to imagine that legislation cannot have the effect of ratifying certain social attitudes. The Sex Discrimination Act and Race Relations Act cannot abolish prejudice, but they do make it less respectable. Section 28, on the other hand, makes prejudice against homosexuals and homosexuality *newly* respectable. Furthermore, as we have seen, it has encouraged an atmosphere of intimidation and completely unnecessary self-censorship within local authorities. The real impact of the Section will be felt in the daily lives of those stigmatised as unacceptable, rather than in the few test cases that are likely to reach the courts.

There is a climate of growing intolerance and hostility towards gay and lesbian men and women in Britain. In a January 1988 Harris poll, the percentage of people who supported the legality of homosexuality fell from its 1985 total of 61% to 48%. A November 1988 British Social Attitudes survey reported that in that year 74% said that homosexual relationships were 'wrong', up from 62% in 1983 and 69% in 1985 (reported in the *Independent*, 3 November 1988). In line with this general hardening of attitudes, 'queerbashing' incidents in London more than doubled in 1987, and in the same year, there were attacks on a dozen gay bars – one with bricks, one by six people armed with teargas and one by a gun-toting mob. In December 1987 the offices of the London weekly gay newspaper *Capital Gay* were set on fire in an arson attack as Section 28 was being debated in Parliament. In an extraordinary outburst on the floor of the House of Commons, Conservative MP Elaine Kellet-Bowman refused to condemn the attack, saying 'It is quite right that there should be an intolerance of evil'. The Conservative Family Campaign (whose patrons include Dame Jill Knight MP, one of the original backers of Section 28, and Geoffrey Dickens MP) wants not only to re-criminalise male homosexuality but to introduce the compulsory 'tagging and isolation' of homosexual people.

In Norway, by complete contrast, national legislation makes it illegal to 'publicly threaten, insult or bear hatred towards, persecute or hold in contempt a person or group on the ground of homosexual orientation or way of life'. Indeed, Britain's quiet

Section 28

approval of bigotry towards homosexuals is most striking when set against the situation in some other European countries. In Norway, and also in the Netherlands, where 7,000 people demonstrated against Section 28 outside the British Embassy, there are laws which expressly prohibit discrimination against lesbians and gay men. In Sweden it is a criminal offence to make derogatory remarks about a person's homosexuality (as it is in relation to race, colour, national or ethnic origin and religious belief). Commercial organisations are forbidden to discriminate on the ground of homosexuality, and gay couples living together share the same rights as heterosexual co-habitees.

One of the most offensive aspects of Section 28 is its description of the family relationship between gay parents and children as a 'pretence'. Many such relationships are considerably more supportive and loving than their heterosexual counterparts, as the statistics on child abuse show, and as was pointed out in both Houses by opponents of the clause. But Section 28 states as a matter of law that local authorities are not allowed to put forward the perfectly sensible notion that such relationships are acceptable as family. This remarkable denial of the reality of thousands of parents' and children's lives will have a particularly damaging effect on these young people, who need reassurance that they and their families are entitled to be treated as equal members of society. Children have a right to know that, whatever their parents' sexuality, they are entitled to be treated the same as everybody else; equally, young people who are beginning to experience their own sexuality as directed towards members of the same gender have a right to be told that this will not devalue them in any way as human beings or as citizens. In addition, it should not be forgotten that there are very many *heterosexual* parents who have in this context demanded *their* right to ensure that their children are not exposed to a climate in schools which encourages hatred and bigotry, whether they grow up to identify themselves as heterosexual or not.

The National Council for Civil Liberties has long since campaigned for, and believed in the right of, citizens to lead the private lives of their choice, regardless of sexual orientation. It has also recognised from the outset that Section 28 represents a threat to civil liberties across the board. It is an attack on the right to a private life, an attack on freedom of choice and freedom of expression, and amounts to a denial of that right to dignity and respect which should be the due of *all* citizens.

The National Council for Civil Liberties believes that Section 28 will increase prejudice and encourage bigotry, and that it constitutes a dangerous precedent which could lead, not only to further restrictions on the public advocacy of lesbian and gay rights, but also to similar measures being directed against other minority groups. In addition, as we have already noted, that the Government should be prepared to support actual legislation on the basis of evidence which, when examined, turns out to be either non-existent or a complete distortion of the truth, is a matter of grave concern. So too is the Catch 22 message which the Government has implicitly sent out to local authorities: 'We are quite happy that you should have non–discrimination and equal opportunity policies, but we are warning you that anything you actually do to further those policies runs the risk of being reinterpreted as an illegal activity.' Whether or not Section 28 will succeed in achieving such a state of paralysis will be borne out by the actions of local authorities in repudiating self-censorship and in continuing to move forward with their equal opportunity and anti–discrimination initiatives.

The National Council for Civil Liberties is concerned to monitor the effects of Section 28 and any reports of these effects should be sent to:

The Legal and Campaign Department
The National Council for Civil Liberties (Liberty)
21 Tabard Street
London SE1 4LA

Section 28

Useful organisations

- Association of London Authorities (ALA)
  36 Old Queen Street
  London SW1 9JE
  tel: 01 222 7799

- Campaign for Homosexual Equality
  PO Box 342 London WC1X OAP
  tel: 01 833 3912

- London Lesbian and Gay Switchboard
  (24 hour telephone helpline)
  tel: 01 837 7324

- Law Centres Federation
  18-19 Warren Street
  London W1P 5DB
  tel: 01 387 8570

- National Council for Civil Liberties (Liberty)
  21 Tabard Street
  London SE1 4LA
  tel: 01 403 3888

- National Association of Citizens Advice Bureaux
  115 Pentonville Road
  London N1 9LZ
  tel: 01 833 2181

- National Union of Teachers (NUT)
  Hamilton House
  Mabledon Place
  London WC1
  tel: 01 388 6191

- National Council for Voluntary Organisations (NCVO)
  26 Bedford Square
  London WC1
  tel: 01 636 4066

- National Union of Students (NUS)
  461 Holloway Road
  London N7
  tel: 01 272 8900

- North West Campaign for Homosexual Equality
  c/o The Gay Centre
  PO Box 153
  Manchester M60 1LP

- OLGA (Organisation of Lesbian and Gay Action)
  PO Box 147
  London WC2H 0BB
  tel: 01 247 1441 ext 22

- Stop The Clause Education group
  c/o OLGA (as above)

- Section 28 Arts Lobby
  c/o Drill Hall Arts Centre
  16 Chenies Street
  London WC1

- Scottish Homosexual Action Group
  38a Broughton Street
  Edinburgh EH1 3SA
  tel: 031 556 8894

Appendix One
Local Government Act 1988

28–(1) The following section shall be inserted after section 2 of the Local Government Act 1986 (prohibition of political publicity) –

2A–(1) A local authority shall not

(a) intentionally promote homosexuality or publish material with the intention of promoting homosexuality.

(b) promote the teaching in any maintained school of the acceptability of homosexuality as a pretended family relationship.

(2) Nothing in subsection (1) above shall be taken to prohibit the doing of anything for the purpose of treating or preventing the spread of disease.

(3) In any proceedings in connection with the application of this section a court shall draw such inferences as to the intention of the local authority as may reasonably be drawn from the evidence before it.

(4) In subsection (1) (b) above 'maintained school' means,

(a) in England and Wales, a county school, voluntary school, nursery school or special school, within the meaning of the Education Act 1944.

(b) in Scotland, a public school, nursery school or special school, within the meaning of the Education (Scotland) Act 1980.

(2) This section shall come into force at the end of the period of two months beginning with the day on which this Act is passed.

Appendix Two
Ministerial statements as recorded in Hansard

All debates during the course of a Bill though Parliament are recorded in the official reports referred to as *Hansard*. Copies of these reports are available from HMSO bookshops or from:

> PO Box 276,
> London SW8 5DT

Telephone orders: 01 622 3316; price £3.25 per copy.

This appendix of extracts from *Hansard* includes only statements made on behalf of the Government. In the House of Commons, the statements were made by **Michael Howard QC, MP,** Minister for Local Government at the Department of the Environment. In the House of Lords, the statements were made by the **Earl of Caithness,** the Government Minister responsible for the Bill in the House of Lords.

On discrimination and equal opportunities

Let me make absolutely clear at the outset that the clause in no way imposes some form of discrimination against homosexuals. The Government are firmly opposed to all forms of discrimination.
(House of Lords, 16.2.88, col. 641.)

The clause is not about stopping local authorities providing services to homosexuals. Some local authorities have tried to ensure that the services provided by the councils serve the needs of homosexuals as much as the needs of the community. There can be no objection to such an aim.
(House of Lords, 2.2.88, col. 1017.)

Noble Lords have not raised the point, but the clause is not about banning the employment of homosexuals by local authorities. Like all public bodies, local authorities should be, and I'm sure are, equal opportunity employers.
(House of Lords, 2.2.88, col. 1018.)

No one is denying that homosexuals are entitled to council services on the same basis as all other electors and ratepayers. There is no case for any public authority discriminating against anyone solely on the grounds of either sexual orientation, or seeking to persuade others to do so.
(House of Lords, 16.2.88, col. 596.)

Section 28

The Government are against discrimination in any form. It is no part of our intention in supporting Clause 28 to remove the right of homosexuals to receive council services. As ratepayers and electors, as a number of noble Lords have pointed out in the debates, they are entitled to have access to those services on the same basis that anyone else does. Nothing in Clause 28 interferes with that right. There is nothing in the clause that would: 'authorise a local authority to discriminate against a person by reason of the sexuality of that person'. The clause limits what a local authority may do. It confers no powers or authority whatsoever. Any claim to the contrary is, quite simply, without foundation.
(House of Lords, 16.2.88, col. 642.)

I re-emphasise that it is no part of the Government's intention in supporting the provision to remove the rights of homosexuals to receive council services. As ratepayers and electors, they are entitled to access to council services on the same basis as anyone else. There is nothing in the provision which would damage that right.
(House of Commons, 9.3.88, col. 420.)

Let me make it plain that it is no part of our intention in supporting this clause to affect the civil rights of any person. We are talking about the use of public money to give preferential treatment to certain people, activities and tendencies. The clause prevents discrimination in favour of a particular purpose – the promotion of homosexuality. Therefore, there is nothing in the clause that would give any local authority any justification for discrimination against homosexuals.
(House of Commons, 9.3.88, col. 424.)

Local authority's 'intention'

I start from the point that we have always been clear that what is prohibited by this clause are those actions which are deliberately carried out by the authority for that purpose. This being so, it follows that no action undertaken by a local authority for any purpose within the authority's powers, untainted by any intention of promoting homosexuality, would be prohibited by the clause.
(House of Lords, 1.2.88, col. 891.)

We have made some important amendments which remove any question that we are concerned with anything but the intention of a local authority in carrying out any activity.
(House of Lords, 16.2.88, col. 597.)

The Government's amendments at Committee Stage, together with those agreed by the House earlier today and yesterday, put it beyond doubt that it is the local authority's intention which is crucial to deciding whether it has acted unlawfully. The fact that the service is provided for the benefit of homosexuals is not material, unless the

local authority's purpose in funding the service is to promote homosexuality.
(House of Lords, 16.2.88, col. 642.)

Libraries, theatre, music licences etc.

Local authorities have a duty to grant music licences and to consider properly applications for music licences in accordance with the law. I am happy to give the Hon. Gentleman the assurance that, in our understanding of the matter, the clause would not, in any way, affect the carrying out by local authorities of those duties.
(House of Commons, 15.12.87, col. 1020.)

Local authorities have a duty to provide a comprehensive library service; provided that this, and this only, is what they are intending to do, there can be no question of the clause inhibiting them from stocking any book that they think necessary for that purpose. Local authorities have power to provide entertainments. Provided that this, and this only, is what they are intending to do, there is no reason why the clause should inhibit them from staging plays by Joe Orton or Oscar Wilde.
(House of Lords, 1.2.88, col. 891.)

I can assure the Committee that it is no part of the Government's intention to inhibit local libraries in their decisions on which books to stock. We recognise that local authorities are under a duty to provide a comprehensive and efficient library service and that they may wish to stock a range of material about homosexuality, dealing with homosexual themes or written by homosexual authors. In our view, Clause 28 does not stop them doing so unless they are setting out intentionally to promote homosexuality.
(House of Lords, 1.2.88, col. 943.)

It needs to decide what its purpose is in either stocking the books or funding the play. If its purpose is to fund a work of literary or artistic merit then its purpose will be legitimate.
(House of Lords, 1.2.88, col. 951.)

A local authority wishing to stage or assist with the staging of plays as part of a programme designed to provide a wide cross section of material for the general public need not feel constrained from doing so by this provision ... However, if the local authority were to promote a succession of plays which promoted homosexuality as their only motive, the plays must be subject to questions that would only be resolved by the courts. It will then become the defence of the local authority to say that it was not their intention ... In summary, the Government do not believe that the local authorities would be prevented by Clause 28 from financing the theatre for the purposes of ensuring that the public have access to a full range of available material.
(House of Lords, 2.2.88, col. 960.)

Section 28

This clause is not about making local authorities into petty censors of the arts. As we have repeatedly said, no local authority will be affected by the clause in its support for the arts, if its aim is simply to provide the inhabitants of its area with access to a full range of literary and artistic work.
(House of Lords, 2.2.88, col. 1017.)

Education (including counselling of pupils)

(Clause 27 below refers to the later Clause, then Section, 28)

The precise purpose of the new Section 2A (i.e. Clause 27) was to put into legislative form the principle set out in the recent Department of Education and Science circular on sex education that homosexuality should not be portrayed as the norm. It is not right that pupils should be taught, in any school, that homosexuality is the norm. It is even less acceptable for local authorities to promote such teaching.
(House of Commons, 15.12.87, col. 1018.)

To suggest that pupils must continue to be given the advice, information and counselling that they need about homosexuality is different from being taught that homosexuality is acceptable as a pretended family relationship. There is nothing in Clause 27 that will prevent the legitimate provision of information, advice or unbiased counselling of pupils, but activities conducted by local authorities in a biased way or in a way that presents as the norm a sexual orientation that is not the norm would be stopped by Clause 27.
(House of Commons, 15.12.87, col. 1019.)

... the clause would in no way prevent local authorities ensuring that parents or children have access to counselling services to provide help in an objective and helpful fashion. That is quite different from intentionally promoting homosexuality, which is what the clause prohibits.
(House of Lords, 1.2.88, col. 890.)

Clearly it is important for a local authority and its staff to feel free to discuss with any pupil any problems that arise because of a pupil's personal preferences, including problems that involve the discussion of homosexuality. The Government naturally share the Opposition's concern that local authorities should not be prevented from ensuring that pupils with personal difficulties have access to persons, be they teachers or specialised counsellors, who can discuss those personal circumstances in an objective and helpful fashion. That is quite different of course from promoting homosexuality or promoting the teaching of the acceptability of homosexuality as a pretended family relationship.
(House of Lords, 1.2.88, col. 966.)

We think that it is right to make it clear on the face of the legislation that local authorities should not be using their limited powers to encourage teaching that portrays homosexual relationships which have the appearance of being family relationships, in most senses of that phrase, as being on those grounds a welcomed development or one to be emulated. We believe that the wording of paragraph 2A(1)(b) expressed this mischief well, that it in no way prevents local authorities from advocating a tolerant and non-discriminatory approach to children living in such relationships and that it in no way interferes with the proper role of teachers.
(House of Lords, 16.2.88, col. 628.)

The paragraph is directed solely at local authorities, not at the teachers. The local authority's only function in this field is now to state its views in a statement under Section 17 of the Education (No.2) Act 1986. As I have explained, the governing body is not bound by that statement. The teacher is answerable to the governing body and not to the local authority.
(House of Lords, 16.2.88, col. 613.)

Voluntary organisations

Local authorities have power to assist voluntary organisations providing public services. If they want to support a homosexual 'help-line', provided that they do so on the same basis that they would support a similar facility for any other section of the community, the clause gives no reason why they should not do so.
(House of Lords, 16.2.88, col. 891.)

The amendment makes it even clearer that where a local authority for a proper purpose within its powers, decides to give assistance to a voluntary group it does not have to conduct an investigation into the motives of that group. It is sufficient that the local authority's own intention is unimpeachable.
(House of Lords, 16.2.88, col. 624.)

Neither is there anything in this clause which would stop a local authority undertaking any activity or service within its powers, or assisting anyone else to do so, simply and solely because that activity or service is aimed at meeting the particular needs of homosexuals. An authority might, for example, wish to finance a voluntary organisation providing counselling and advice services to homosexuals; it is entitled to contribute to the funds of non-profit-making bodies providing a public service – under Section 137(3) of the Local Government Act 1972 – if it thinks it appropriate to do so. The National Council for Voluntary Organisations has written to me and no doubt to other noble Lords, suggesting that this clause will prevent the funding in the future of a number of groups offering services for homosexuals. I can reassure it that there is no reason why this should be the case provided that the intention of the local authority is to provide or support a service and the funding is within their powers.

An argument to the contrary could not be sustained by reference to the wording of the clause. The fact that the existence of such services might encourage people to use them is irrelevant. What is relevant, and the only thing that is relevant, is the purpose of the local authority in funding the service, not any unpredicted or incidental effect of their doing so.
(House of Lords, 16.2.88, col. 642.)

For example, the question has been raised whether it will continue to be open to local authorities to fund Gay Bereavement, a counselling service for homosexuals whose partner has died. If a local authority perceives a genuine need for such a service on grounds relevant to one of its powers to support voluntary organisations, and having weighed all its priorities, decides that it is right to offer assistance to the service at public expense, it is entitled to do so. A court could find the authority in breach of the prohibition only if having looked at all the circumstances of the grant, it could reasonably be held that the authority had funded the service in order to promote homosexuality. This does not, of course, mean that a local authority would not have to tread very carefully in taking a decision to fund a service designed exclusively for homosexuals. It would have to be satisfied that its action could in no way be construed as promoting homosexuality.

A court might well infer that an authority that gave assistance to Gay Bereavement but refused to give such assistance to CRUSE – the organisation that provides a similar support for widows – might have to face questions about its motives.
(House of Lords, 16.2.88, col. 642.)

Health education and counselling

Care, counselling and health education on AIDS and other diseases are part of the treatment or the prevention of the spread of disease.
(House of Commons, 15.12.87, col. 1019.)

We believe that care, counselling, and health education in relation to AIDS or other diseases are fully covered by the present formulation in subsection (2), as are all other activities concerned with the prevention of disease.
(House of Lords, 1.2.88, col. 893.)

I make it clear that subsection (2) puts beyond doubt that anything done to prevent the spread of disease is in no way affected by the clause. That of course includes matters such as the road show the Terrence Higgins Trust Road Show] ...
(House of Lords, 16.2.88, col. 638.)

Appendix Three
Government Circular 12/88

Circular 12/88
(Department of the Environment)
Circular 16/88
(Welsh Office)

Joint Circular from the Department of the Environment
2 Marsham Street, London SW1P 3EB
Welsh Office
Cathays Park, Cardiff CF1 3NQ

20 May 1988

Local Government Act 1988

1. We are directed by the Secretary of State for the Environment and the Secretary of State for Wales to refer to the Local Government Act 1988 which received Royal Assent on 24 March 1988. This circular provides general guidance on the Act's provisions.

[paragraphs 2-17 omitted]

18. Section 28 adds a new section 2A to the Local Government Act 1986 to prohibit local authorities from promoting homosexuality. This section will come into force on 24 May 1988.

19. Section 2A(1)(a) prohibits a local authority from intentionally promoting homosexuality, or from publishing material with the intention of promoting homosexuality. The provision will be relevant in cases where a local authority, in exercising one of its statutory functions, proposes to do something for the deliberate purpose of promoting homosexuality. Local authorities will not be prevented by this section from offering the full range of their services to homosexuals, on the same basis as to all their inhabitants. So long as they are not setting out to promote homosexuality, they may, for example, include in their public libraries books and periodicals about homosexuality, or written by homosexuals, and fund theatre and other arts events which may include homosexual themes.

20. Section 2A(1)(a) highlights one particular aspect of promoting homosexuality that has given rise to concern. It specifically prohibits a local authority, in exercising its statutory functions, from promoting the teaching in any maintained school of the acceptability of homosexuality as a pretended family relationship. The effect of this

will be that a local authority will be prohibited from promoting homosexuality in the expression of its policy on sex education. Responsibility for sex education continues to rest with school governing bodies, by virtue of Section 18 of the Education (No.2) Act 1986. Section 28 does not affect the activities of school governors, nor of teachers. It will not prevent the objective discussion of homosexuality in the classroom, nor the counselling of pupils concerned about their sexuality. Such activities will continue to be governed by Section 46 of the Education (No.2) Act 1986. Guidance on this, and on the Government's policy on sex education at school, is provided in DES Circular, 11/87. Section 46 provides that where sex education is given 'it should be given in such a manner as to encourage ... pupils to have due regard to moral considerations and the value of family life'. Paragraph 22 of the Circular makes clear the Government's view that there is no place in any school in any circumstances for teaching which advocates homosexual behaviour, which presents it as the norm, or which encourages homosexual experimentation by pupils.

21. Section 2A(2) makes clear that nothing in Section 2A(1) prevents anything being done for the purpose of treating or preventing the spread of disease. Thus, activities in the counselling, health care and health education fields undertaken for the purpose of treating or preventing the spread of disease, including AIDS, will not be prohibited. This includes activities concerned exclusively with the needs of homosexuals.

22. Section 2A(3) states that in any proceedings in connection with the application of this section a court shall draw such inferences as to the intention of the local authority as may reasonably be drawn from the evidence before it. This is a declaratory statement of the fact that a court considering a case against a local authority on the grounds that it has intentionally promoted homosexuality will be required to have regard to all the relevant circumstances of the case, on the basis of the evidence before it.

Enquiries

23. Enquiries on Section 28 should be addressed (in England) to: LGIB Division, Department of the Environment, 2 Marsham Street, London SW1P 3EB
and (in Wales) to: WEPD Division, LG Branch, Welsh Office, Crown Buildings, Cathays Park, Cardiff CF1 3NQ.

Appendix Four
Letters from Ministers in relation to Section 28

Department of the Environment
2 Marsham Street
London SW1P 3EB
8 February 1988

Dear Mr King,

Thank you for your letter of 12 December 1987 about the provisions of the Local Government Bill prohibiting the promotion of homosexuality by local authorities. I am sorry that you have not had an earlier reply.

The Government is against discrimination in any form, and shares your view that homosexuals should not be unfairly treated in the provision of local authority services. The new provisions were introduced because of the growing concern in Parliament and in the country as a whole about the use of ratepayers' money by some local authorities to promote homosexuality and to encourage teachers to present, as the norm, a sexual orientation which clearly is not the norm. There can be no justification for local authorities using public money intentionally to promote homosexuality. The Government therefore considered it right to support the back–bench amendment to the Local Government Bill, so that such promotion is outlawed in the future. The Labour Party have said that they support the intention behind the amendment.

There has in recent weeks been a significant amount of misrepresentation about the effects of the new provisions. There is nothing in the clause which would prevent local authorities providing information, advice, counselling or any other service to homosexuals on the same basis as to other groups. The new clause includes a sub-section which specifically excludes from the prohibition 'the doing of anything for the purposes of treating or preventing the spread of disease'. Thus the activities of local authorities in providing counselling and health care, for example, in the battle against AIDS will be unaffected by the proposed legislation. In addition, the objective discussion of homosexuality in the classroom will not be affected.

Yours sincerely

P. R. King Esq.

Christopher Chope

Section 28

Department of the Environment
2 Marsham Street
London SW1

Leicester Women's Centre,
94, Belgrave Gate,
Leicester
LE1 3GR

25 March 1988

Dear Madam,

I have been asked to thank you for your recent letter about Clause 28 of the Local Government Bill, the prohibition of the promotion of homosexuality by local authorities. The Local Government Act received the Royal Assent on 24 March.

The Government are against discrimination in any form. It was no part of their intention in supporting this legislation to remove the rights of homosexuals; as ratepayers and electors they are entitled to receive council services on the same basis as everyone else. Nothing in Section 28 would damage this right.

The provisions were introduced because of the growing concern in Parliament and in the country as a whole about the use of ratepayers' money in some local authorities to promote homosexuality. In particular, there was a real concern that local authorities were targetting some activities on young people, in schools and outside, in an apparent endeavour to glamorise homosexuality. Not unnaturally, parents have become increasingly worried and resentful about public money being used in this way to influence the attitudes and behaviour of impressionable young people. The Government believes there can be no justification for local authorities using public money for this purpose.

There has in recent months been a considerable amount of misrepresentation about the effects of the new provisions. There is no question of their leading to a censorship of the arts; preventing local authorities from granting entertainment licences; banning books stocked in public libraries as part of the normal library function; stopping activities in health care and counselling; discouraging the balanced and objective discussion of homosexuality in the classroom; or providing any other service to homosexuals on the same basis as to other groups. Neither will the provisions stop the useful work that has been done by local authorities in the fight against AIDS: there is a specific exclusion for anything done for the purpose of treating or preventing the spread of disease.

In summary, the Government considers that no legitimate activities will be stopped; Section 28 will only apply to local authorities who set out deliberately to promote homosexuality.

Yours faithfully

N. Cook

LOCAL GOVERNMENT 1 DIVISION

Department of Education and Science
Elizabeth House
York Road
London SE1 7PH
Telephone 01-934 9000
From the Minister of State

Madeleine Colvin
Legal Officer
National Council for Civil Liberties
21 Tabard Street
LONDON SE1 4LA

21 January 1988

Dear Miss Colvin

Thank you for your letter of 8 December to Kenneth Baker concerning Dame Jill Knight's amendment to the Local Government Bill.

The precise terms of the new clause, in as much as it relates to schools, are that a local authority shall not promote the teaching in any maintained school of the acceptability of homosexuality as a pretended family relationship by the publication of material or otherwise. This as you can see relates directly to the activities of local authorities rather than schools. There is a good reason for this. As Michael Howard pointed out at Committee Stage and at Report Stage of the Local Government Bill, a number of local authorities have persisted in recommending to parents and teachers the use of wholly offensive and inappropriate materials relating to homosexuality for use in schools. We consider therefore that the new clause will strengthen the existing requirement placed on local authorities by Section 46 of the Education (No. 2) Act to ensure that whatever sex education is given in schools has regard to 'moral considerations and the value of family life'.

Section 28

There is absolutely no reason why the clause should encourage a climate of intolerance towards homosexuals. It does not prevent balanced and factual teaching about homosexuality taking place in schools, nor does it prevent sensitive counselling of pupils. Rather it is designed to prevent biased and offensive propaganda. I find it most disturbing that much of the opposition to the clause has failed to acknowledge the distasteful nature of the materials distributed by some local authorities.

It is of course right that schools should not foster intolerance in young people. But it is not the job of schools or teachers to take an adversarial stance on the subject of homosexuality, given that many parents regard homosexual practice as not morally acceptable. Schools should not be pressed to adopt such a stance, and it is such encouragement by local authorities that the legislation is intended to prevent.

As you are probably aware, responsibility for determining whether, and if so how, sex education is provided in schools was transferred to the school governors by Section 18(2) of the Education (No.2) Act 1986. We have every confidence that they will exercise their responsibilities for sex education with care and discretion. The new clause will ensure that they will not come under pressure from local authorities to provide inappropriate sex education for pupils.

I am copying this letter to Michael Howard at the Department of Environment.

Yours sincerely

Angela Rumbold

[addressee unknown]

10 Downing Street
London SW1A 2AA

3 March 1988

Dear Sir,

Thank you for your letter of 6 January about the provisions of the Local Government Bill prohibiting the promotion of homosexuality by local authorities.

The Government is against discrimination in any form, and it is no part of our intention in supporting Clause 28 to remove the rights of homosexuals; as ratepayers and electors they are entitled to receive council services on the same basis as everyone else. There is nothing in the clause that would damage this right, and allegations to that effect are quite without foundation.

These provisions were introduced because of the growing concern in Parliament and in the country as a whole about the use of ratepayers' money by some local authorities intentionally to promote homosexuality. In particular, there was a real concern that local authorities were targeting some activities on young people in schools and outside, in an apparent endeavour to glamorise homosexuality. Not unnaturally, parents have become increasingly worried and resentful about public money being used in this way to influence the attitudes and behaviour of impressionable young people. The Government shares the view of the sponsors of this clause that there can be no justification for local authorities using public money for this purpose.

There can be no doubt that these activities have provoked considerable public disquiet. Clause 28 would ensure that this undesirable development could not continue. In our view, removing this source of disquiet will go far to alleviate the resentment which was building up and having a growing and adverse effect on tolerance and understanding.

I consider such incidents such as the attack on the offices of *Capital Gay* to be intolerable. Michael Howard, the Minister of State for Local Government, took the opportunity at the debate on Clause 28 in the House of Commons on 15 December 1987, to state the Government's unqualified condemnation of this incident.

Section 28

I have taken careful note of your remarks on the Press and the right to reply. I know, probably more than most, of the difficulties and hurt which unfair and inaccurate reporting can cause. But there are already a number of bodies which consider complaints about the written press and media, and these bodies can provide for publishing their findings where appropriate. I do not think there would be any real advantage to be gained by legislating in an area like this.

Yours sincerely

Margaret Thatcher

Office of Arts and Libraries
Horse Guards Road
London SW1P 3AL

Telephone 01-279 5929
From the Minister for the Arts

Councillor R. Hughes
Chairman
Arts, Recreation and Tourism Committee
Association of Metropolitan Authorities
35 Great Smith Street
Westminster
LONDON SW1P 3BJ

11 April 1988

Dear Mr Hughes

I thought we had a useful and constructive meeting on 23 March. In the course of it, I undertook to let you have my detailed comments on Section 28 of what is now the Local Government Act.

As I said during the meeting, the section in its final form focuses very clearly on intention, and makes clear that the relevant intention is that of the local authority and not that of the artists, writers, lecturers or other persons whose work the local authority may exhibit or cause to be performed or published.

I have been advised that, in drawing inferences as to intention, a court could be expected to pay regard to the general policy and practice of the local authority. If, for example, an authority clearly had a policy of seeking to bring the work of all sorts of artists and playwrights before the public, and from time to time put on exhibitions or plays for this purpose, the fact that the artists concerned included some who were homosexual would not put the local authority at risk under the section. The local authority's intention would clearly be the promotion of art rather than the promotion of homosexuality.

The same considerations apply to the provision of books. If an authority stocks books of every kind in its libraries, the fact that a particular book deals with the topic of homosexuality, or is written by a homosexual, does not put the authority at risk.

Clearly, I can only reflect the Government's intentions in what I say. I accept that there is always the possibility that somebody will seek to bring a case against an authority, however flimsy the case might be. But that would be so, whatever amendment the Government might have made, and we are firmly of the view that we have safeguarded local authorities against any legal action based on ordinary and reasonable provision for the artistic and literary needs of the population.

I am following up some other points you raised at the meeting and I will let you know the outcome. Meanwhile you are welcome to circulate this letter around your members as you see fit.

Yours sincerely

Richard Luce

Index

Section 28

Liberty

National Council For Civil Liberties

Charter of Civil Rights and Liberties

We are committed to the defence and extension of civil liberties in the United Kingdom and to the rights and freedoms recognised by international law. In particular we are pledged to ensure and safeguard these essential rights:

1. To live in freedom and safe from personal harm.

2. To protection from ill-treatment or punishment that is inhuman or degrading.

3. To equality before the law and to freedom from discrimination on such grounds as disability, political or any other opinion, race, religion, sex, or sexual orientation.

4. To protection from arbitrary arrest and unnecessary detention, the right to a fair, speedy and public trial, to be presumed innocent until proven guilty, and to legal advice and representation.

5. To a fair hearing before any authority exercising power over the individual.

6. To freedom of thought, conscience and belief.

7. To freedom of speech and publication.

8. To freedom of peaceful assembly and association.

9. To move freely within one's country of residence and to leave and enter it without hindrance.

10. To privacy and the right of access to official information.

Liberty Publications

CIVIL LIBERTY BRIEFINGS (all priced at £1.00 inclusive of p&p)

Police & Criminal Evidence Act
Police Accountability
The Conservative Government's Record on Civil Liberties
Travellers on the Road
Public Order Act
The Privacy Implications of the Poll Tax
Your Right to See Your File
The Employment Bill 1987
The Official Secrets Act
The UK Record on Civil Liberties
Identity Cards and the Threat to Civil Liberties
A Bill of Rights
Freedom of Expression in the UK
Prisoners' Rights
Report on the Security Service Bill
Background Paper on Pornography and Censorship

GENERAL (Please add 70p per title to cover p&p; orders of £10 and over, post-free)

We Protest – The Public Order Debate: Peter Thornton	£ 3.95
Trade Unionists & Public Order: Marie Staunton	£ 1.50
Free to Walk Together: Marie Staunton	£ 1.50
Changing Contempt of Court: Andrew Nicol & Heather Rogers	£ 1.20
The National Council for Civil Liberties – The First 50 Years: Mark Lilly	£ 5.95
The Purging of the Civil Service	£ 0.95
Civil Rights for Civil Servants	£ 0.95
Public Order Law: Peter Thornton	£11.95
Stonehenge	£ 1.95
Fire Under the Carpet – Civil Liberties in the 1930s: Sylvia Scaffardi	£ 4.95
Gay Workers, Trade Unions & The Law: Chris Beer, Roland Jeffery & Terry Munyard	£ 1.75
Section 28 – A Practical Guide to the Law & its Implications	£ 4.50
Decade of Decline – Civil Liberties in the Thatcher Years: Peter Thornton	£ 3.95
Penguin/Liberty Guide to Your Rights: Malcolm Hurwitt & Peter Thornton	£ 4.99

POLICING AND CRIMINAL PROCEDURE

Called to Account – The Case for Police Accountability in England & Wales: Sarah Spencer:	£ 3.95
Civil Liberties in the Miners' Dispute (Independent Enquiry Report)	£ 1.50
Poor Law: Ros Franey	£ 1.95
A Fair Cop: Patricia Hewitt	£ 1.75
Southall – 23 April 1979 (Independent Enquiry Report)	£ 2.20
Death of Blair Peach (Independent Enquiry Report)	£ 1.50
Operation Fire/Operation Tan	£ 1.25

NORTHERN IRELAND

Strip Searching – Women Remand Prisoners at Armagh Prison 1982-1985: NCCL Report	£ 1.95
The New Prevention of Terrorism Act 1984. Catherine Scorer, Sarah Spencer & Patricia Hewitt	£ 2.50
The Gibraltar Report – Independent Observer's Report on the Gibraltar Enquiry: Hilary Kitchin	£ 4.00

PRIVACY

Whose File is it Anyway?: Ruth Cohen	£ 2.25
Data Protection: Roger Cornwell & Marie Staunton	£ 3.95
The Zircon Affair: Peter Thornton	£ 0.95

WOMENS' RIGHTS

Positive Action for Women: Paddy Stamp & Sadie Robarts	£ 4.95
Judging Women: Polly Pattullo	£ 0.95
No More Peanuts: Jo Morris	£ 2.50
Amending the Equality Laws: Catherine Scorer & Ann Sedley	£ 0.95
The Rape Controversy: Melissa Benn, Anna Coote & Tess Gill	£ 1.50
Sexual Harassment at Work: Ann Sedley & Melissa Benn	£ 0.95
Maternity Rights at Work: Jean Coussins, Lyn Durward & Ruth Evans	£ 1.50
Women Won't Benefit: Hilary Land & Sue Ward	£ 1.95
The Shiftwork Swindle: Jean Coussins	£ 0.60
The Equality Report: Jean Coussins	£ 1.20
The Unequal Breadwinner: Ruth Lister & Les Wilson	£ 0.35

RACE, NATIONALITY & IMMIGRATION

Race Relations Rights: Paul Gordon, John Wright & Patricia Hewitt	£ 1.95
British Nationality: Ann Dummett & Ian Martin	£ 2.95

Liberty

(National Council for Civil Liberties)

Membership or Affiliation

Individual Members

Individual Membership	£14
Any two people at the same address	£18
Students, OAPs, Claimants	£ 6
Any two students, OAPs or Claimants at the same address	£10
Prisoners	£ 3

Organisations

Under 100 Members	£17
251-500 Members	£30
101-250 Members	£20
501-1000 Members	£40
Over 1000 Members: Details on Application	

I/We enclose a cheque/PO for £...........membership/affiliation and £...........and £...........donation: Total £............

☐ I/We* do/do not require a receipt

I/We accept the aims and the constitution of **Liberty**. I/We* do not/Our organisation* does not have objectives which are incompatible with those of **Liberty**, nor am I/are we* member(s) or part of any organisation whose objectives are incompatible with **Liberty**.*

*Delete where applicable.

Signature ....Date ....

Name..

Organisation

(if affiliate) ....

Address ....

....

☐ Please send me details of direct debit payment
☐ Please send my/our details to a local **Liberty** group

*A copy of the constitution is available from **Liberty***

National Council for Civil Liberties, Freepost, 21 Tabard Street, London SE1 6BP.